EVERYTHING U NEED 2 KNOW

2 Write

A NOVEL

&

Get published

A-Z

June Loves

Author of *The Shelly Beach Writers' Group*

Published in Australia in 2015 by
Loves Books Publishing
PO Box 672, Rye 3941
juneloves@bigpond.com
www.juneloves.com

First published in Australia 2015
Copyright © June Loves 2015

National Library of Australia Cataloguing-in-Publication entry
Creator: Loves, June, 1938- author.
Title: Everything u need 2 know 2 write a novel & get it published:
       A-Z / June Loves.
ISBN: 9780994208002 (paperback)
Notes: Includes index.
Subjects: Fiction--Authorship--Handbooks, manuals, etc.
Fiction--Technique--Handbooks, manuals, etc.
Manuscript preparation (Authorship)--Handbooks, manuals, etc.
Dewey Number: 808.397

Cover design by Denys Marrow
Book formatting and layout by Nelly Murariu

About the Author

June Loves is the author of over 100 books, including non-fiction and fiction for adults and children, reference books and academic publications. She has been a newspaper journalist, freelance writer, teacher, librarian and bookseller. She lives near the beach in Victoria, Australia with her husband. Her latest books are *The Shelly Beach Writers' Group* and *Modern Grandparenting.*

*For my husband Max and
our ever-expanding beautiful family.*

Acknowledgments

I would like to thank the following people:

* My micro-managing editor, **Amanda Spedding** who has so painstakingly edited the entries from the fictional members of the Shelly Beach Writers' Group and spent hours editing the index with her microscopic eye. And for her excellent advice re Essential Books for Your Library.

* My caring publishing and marketing consultant **Julie Postance.**

* My book designer, **Nelly Murariu,** for her brilliant book design that is so Shelly Beach.

* **My husband,** my loving, walking, talking thesaurus and dictionary and our big beautiful family who were always available to check the entries from the Shelly Beach Writers' Group members.

* And my **Writers' Group** who in no way resemble the Shelly Beach Writers' Group.

Contents

✳ Letter Entries ✳

A Note From the Editor

Everything U Need 2 Know 2 Write a Novel & Get Published: A-Z is a collection written by the SBWG (Shelly Beach Writers' Group). The members of the SBWG chose the A-Z entries by brainstorming topics, writing the topic names on post-its, and placing the post-its in a jar. Members then selected the entries they wanted to write about from the jar. If a member felt they were lacking in expertise for a particular entry they replaced their choice and selected another. Members' first names at the end of entries acknowledge authorship.

See and See also references

See and *See also* references allow readers to cross-reference. For example: Agent [*See Literary Agent*]; DIY publishing [*See also e-book, e-publishing path, self-publishing*]

Useful Tips

Useful tips contributed by members of the Shelly Beach Writers' Group.

Editor's Disclaimer

Thank you in advance if you noted an inconsistency or small error. Considering the English language and the global publishing industry are in a constant state of flux—forever changing—what is correct today may be incorrect tomorrow.

Violet Harris
Editor

Meet the Shelly Beach Writers' Group members

Josh Colovich is Shelly Beach's enthusiastic young teacher. He's resurrected his Young Adult speculative novel he began at university. His broken romance with fellow member Bianca, allowed him plenty of time to build on his 30,000-word manuscript. (Now Bianca and Josh are married he still finds time to write is an issue.)

Bianca Jones-Colovich is owner of Scissors Salon. She's writing a romantic, sexy chick-lit novel set in New York—similar to *Romeo and Juliet* except her two main characters don't die. Keeping the frisson frissoning is a challenge for Bianca.

Violet Harris is the editor of *Everything U Need 2 Know 2 Write a Novel & Get Published: A-Z*. Her first novel *The Compost Bin Murder* is published. She's completed six Agatha-Christie type *whodunits*, which are stored under the cats' sofa. She's working on her seventh *whodunit—The Well Murder* (working title). Violet has years and years of experience in the book industry, working in her late father's printing and publishing business. She is contemplating self-publishing.

Bill Kruger is a short-listed author and tutor of the Shelly Beach Writers' Group. His first novel was a success and short-listed for a prestigious literary prize. His second novel was released last year with mid-list sales. Bill uses his car and the surf beach as a writing place. Deb, Bill's wife, has returned to teaching so they can afford to rent a bigger house. Bill is working on his third novel while caring for Hunter, their three-year-old son.

Gina Laurel is key keeper and coordinator for the Shelly Beach Writers' Group. Her duties consist of opening and closing the community hall, turning the heater on and off, preparing tea, coffee, and supper. Other duties include liaising with the tutor, and photocopying or emailing whatever is required for the next meeting. Gina is working with her agent on the revision of her contemporary novel.

Pandora Papadopolous is a former high-profile spin-doctor who's made a sea change to Shelly Beach. She manages her Beach Writers' Retreat and is happy to pass on her PR expertise to members. Pandora is writing unconnected short pieces, which could be the start of a *payback novel.*

Dr Digby Prentice-Hill (a literary, not a medical doctor) is a semi-retired academic. He planned to write a tell-all memoir. Now (because of legal ramifications) he's writing a psychological thriller set in academia.

Daphne Schwarz is Shelly Beach's prominent *green* activist and feature editor for the *Sea Haven Sentinel* (local paper). She's researching the Regency period in anticipation of writing a Regency romance. She also writes *green* articles for city newspapers and magazines, posts for blogs and websites.

Lee Wang, former chef at Shelly Beach Pub, wrote his blockbuster, action-packed crime fiction novel—which is now with a mainstream publisher—between his chef shifts. His novel centres on murder and vice in the Hong Kong kitchen of a five-star hotel. Lee is completing his medical degree in the city and writing in what little is left of his spare time. If the mainstream publisher doesn't pick up his novel he's going to self-publish.

A

a and an [See also The]

A and *an* are essential, simple words known grammatically as indefinite articles.

* Use *a* before words beginning with a consonant, or a vowel sounding like a consonant. For example: a writer, a eulogy, and a unicorn.
* Use *an* before words beginning with a vowel, a consonant that sounds like a vowel or a consonant that is not sounded at all. For example: an ostrich, an author, an heir.
* Use *a* and *an* with singular nouns. For example: There is a seagull. There is an editor.

Sound is the key to choosing *a* or *an* before figures, acronyms and abbreviations. For example: a 200-hectare property, a VIP lounge, an ASIO file, a $9000 diamond ring.

Traditionally *an* was often used before words beginning with *h* if the first syllable was unstressed and the h sound dropped. For example: an hotel, an historian, an honourable man. Today it's common to sound the *h* in words and use *a* before them. DIGBY

Watch you don't use a or an before an unaccountable noun. i.e. a sand X, a salt X.

abbreviations

Abbreviations are words that are shortened i.e. when you use a few letters instead of the whole word. Abbreviations are mostly used in titles, addresses, business names, tables, charts, maps, directories, and footnotes. For example: e.g. means for example. BIANCA

> *Check publishers' guidelines for accepted abbreviations before submitting your novel.*

abstract noun [See also Concrete noun]

Abstract nouns are words for names of stuff that have no physical existence. They are names of ideas and things we can feel or imagine. For example: love, failure, jealousy, betrayal and victory. JOSH

acknowledgements [See also Back matter/Dedication/Front matter]

Acknowledgements is a headed section of text usually found among the front or end pages of your novel. You can write one or more lines, paragraphs, or pages and pages of acknowledgements where you acknowledge everyone you can think of in the writing and publishing of your novel—even pets. Check you're using the correct spelling when you name people and watch you don't duplicate people you mention in your dedication. VIOLET

> *A thank you to hard-working research assistants, long-suffering agents, and editors is always appreciated especially if you're thinking of writing another novel.*

acronym

Acronym is a word formed by the first letters (or word parts) of other words. For example: SBWG (Shelly Beach Writers'

Group), CIA (Central Intelligence Agency), CD (Compact Disk). Always explain the acronym after the first mention. Use the letters following with the full words in brackets. DIGBY

Beware of littering your novel with a confusing overload of acronyms so your reader loses the plot. This is particularly relevant if you're writing a novel about political intrigue in government departments.

acquisition meetings

Acquisition meetings are held by publishing companies to decide which manuscripts they will accept for publishing. Not only do your agent and editor need to love your novel, but the sales, marketing and publicity personnel must also be wildly enthusiastic about it. They must want to publish your novel and take you on as an author. BILL

Acquisition meetings are usually held weekly but it may take a while for an editor to get all the necessary data together for your novel to be presented. Obviously acquisition meetings will not concern you if you're self-publishing.

active voice [See also Grammar/Passive voice /Verb]

Active voice is a grammatical term. Writing using active voice has active verbs and sentences where the subject performs the action. For example: The dog buried her novel. Lee lost his plot. When writers use active voice it makes their writing vital and vigorous and it keeps a novel moving along. GINA

adage

Adage is a traditional saying that is generally accepted as being true. For example: Don't give up your day job. And writing is 80 per cent perspiration and 20 per cent inspiration. VIOLET

The above adages equate to excellent advice for aspiring novelists.

adjective [See also Parts of speech]

An adjective is a word that modifies (tells more about) a noun, a pronoun or another adjective. Adjectives describe the colour, size, number or any other aspect of a noun, pronoun or another adjective. For example: The persistent writer completed his novel. VIOLET

Choose adjectives with care for your novel. Don't over-egg them.

advance [See also Contract]

An advance is an amount of money that mainstream, small and independent publishers pay writers before a book is published. The advance is deducted from earned royalties from sales of the finished novel. BILL

In the current digital publishing climate advances are dwindling— or vanishing altogether. However, some much-awarded and widely-published authors can still receive six-figure advances so don't give up hope.

adverb [See also Parts of speech]

An adverb is a word that modifies (tells more about) a verb, an adjective or another adverb. For example: The writers' group meeting was unbelievably boring. Too many adverbs can make for melodrama. Edit unnecessary adverbs as you write, have your pen in hand to erase or your finger on the delete button. VIOLET

If you choose the right verb you don't need an adverb.

afterword [See also Back matter/Endnotes]

Afterword is the one-two pages of text written by the author at the end of a book. A popular novel is usually devoid of an Afterword—however it could be included if a publisher or author wishes to do so. DIGBY

agent [See Literary Agent]

agented material

Agented material is submissions from literary agents to a publisher. Some publishing companies, especially larger ones, only accept agented material. PANDORA

airport novel [See also Plane book]

An airport novel is a bulky novel, usually purchased at airport bookshops and packed with action, suspense and sex to break the boredom of long-haul flights. Readers buy airport novels to read while they're crammed into a metal-enclosed shoebox to travel in space. Airport novels are also useful reads when you're stranded in an airport or while your plane waits on the tarmac for the co-pilot who slept in after a wild night on the town. Fantasising that your novel will be a bestseller in an airport bookshop can help in getting to the finishing line when you're writing your novel. PANDORA

Survival novels do not make good airport reads.

a.k.a/aka

a.k.a./aka is an abbreviation for *also known as*. The modern trend is to write *aka* without full stops. DIGBY

Consult publishers' guidelines or be consistent in your use of punctuation if you are self-publishing.

allegory

An allegory is a story that is simple on the surface, but has a deeper, darker meaning or voice underneath. You can use allegoric principles in your novel to represent facets of life. If Louisa May Alcott's *Little Women* was a fave read when you were young, you may be unaware of its allegoric representation taken from John Bunyan's *Pilgrim's Progress* and just love the novel for Jo—the young, spunky-writer protagonist. DAPHNE

alliteration [See also Figures of speech]

Alliteration is the repeated use of the beginning consonant sound of words in a sentence or phrase. You can use alliteration to make your writing sound more poetic. Sometimes alliteration occurs in your novel without you thinking about it. For example: The Dog doggedly dawdled all the way home. GINA

ampersand (&)

Ampersand (&) is a typographical symbol that indicates *and*. It is found above the number 7 on the querty keyboard or you can scribble it by hand in your notes. An ampersand is not usually used in the text of a novel unless it's part of a trade name or title. PANDORA

anagram

An anagram is a word formed by mixing up the letters of another word. For example: tale is an anagram of late. DIGBY

and [See also Conjunction/Transitions]

And is a connecting word—a conjunction. Using *and* reinforces the words before, or emphasises words following. Today it's acceptable to begin a sentence with *and*. In the past it was frowned upon. LEE

Don't overuse and. Too many long sentences using and can make your writing tedious.

anecdote

An anecdote is a short, often funny re-telling of an incident. For example: students were asked to write opening sentences for their novels. Their tutor said, *Religion, royalty, sex, money, and crime sell popular novels.* So a student wrote an opening line for her blockbuster novel. *OmahGod!* said the Duchess to her lover. *My priceless jewels have been stolen.* VIOLET

Anecdotes are useful to collect and use in your novel.

anon [See also Pen name]

The word anon indicates that the author is unknown. Using *anon* was a fashion in the late eighteenth and nineteenth centuries, partly because of the stigma attached to writing fiction as an occupation—especially for women writers.

An author rarely uses anonymity today. With global access to information it's practically impossible to practise anonymity successfully. GINA

Anonymity can be useful as a gimmicky marketing tool.

antagonist [See also Protagonist]

The antagonist is the character in your novel that opposes, competes or is against your protagonist. Antagonists can be humans, vampires, ghosts, aliens—whatever. Intriguing antagonists make for page-turning plots. JOSH

anthropomorphism

Anthropomorphism occurs when a writer gives an animal, bird or insect character human feelings. For example: when a dog becomes a confidante for his owner. GINA

antonym [See also Synonym/Thesaurus]

An antonym is a word that is opposite in meaning to another word. For example: fast/slow, young/old. JOSH

aphorism

An aphorism is a short clever saying expressing a general truth i.e. you cannot write the next chapter of your life while you're still rereading the last chapter. BIANCA

An aphorism is only an aphorism if the reader understands that it's a clever saying expressing a general truth.

apostrophe
[See also Contraction/The Greengrocer's apostrophe/Punctuation]

An apostrophe—the flying comma—is a punctuation mark that causes a great amount of grief to writers. Apostrophe police delight in spotting the inappropriate use of apostrophes. An apostrophe is used to show when a letter or letters are missing i.e. don't = do not, or with the letter s to show who owns something. For example: The Dog's feelings were hurt. An area of confusion also arises when an apostrophe is added to a surname ending in the letter s. For example: Jones's house or Jones' house. Inappropriate use of apostrophes can cause excitement and angst, however the apostrophe is losing its force and is being dropped from place names, signs et cetera. There's a camp that wants to abolish apostrophes completely. JOSH

Possessive pronouns like theirs and its do not use apostrophes.

ARC

ARC is an acronym for Advanced Reader Copy. An ARC is an advanced copy of a book sent out for promotion and reviews. LEE

ARC is not to be confused with arc, which is the shape of the story and/or elements in your novel.

arc [See also Character arc]

An arc (not to be confused with Noah's ark) refers to the shape and/or elements in your novel. An arc occurs when you build one event after another event until there's a climax or resolution in your novel. Then it is said that your writing takes the shape of an arc. LEE

archetype [See also Characters/Plot]

Archetype is a word that means the original model or form. The adjective *archetypal* is frequently used in writerly discussion. Archetypal narratives are used to describe the classical story arc of tragedy or a novel written as a quest narrative. Archetypal characters can be typical, conventional or classical characters e.g. tragic lovers, solve-it-all sleuths, blood-sucking vampires or the hero on a quest. An archetypal plot can refer to a typical or conventional plot relating to the genre or type of novel. **DAPHNE**

Aristotle's 3-act structure [See also Protagonist]

Aristotle's 3-act structure for a story of a beginning, middle and an end is frequently adapted to contemporary fiction plots.

* **Act 1** has an engaging opening, which foreshadows the conflict and propels the story forward. The main character's goal is established. The First Plot Point (or turning point) establishes the conflict the novel is trying to resolve.

* **Act 2** comprises the bulk of the story—about ½ to ¾ of the book. It contains the Second Plot Point and should immediately spin the story into the middle. The middle consists of rising action and conflicts that create obstacles or challenges to thwart the main character. These climb in importance or intensity as they lead to the climax. Depending on the length of the novel, the main character (protagonist) should face three to seven obstacles or challenges. Each should be more difficult for the protagonist to overcome. The story will be tighter if the resolution of one obstacle creates another. The climax determines whether the protagonist wins or loses. The protagonist can fail or figure out how to turn things around.

* **Act 3** (the end or denouement) has falling action in which the story winds down. Final revelations and loose ends are tied up. After the climax in Act 2, there's a major revelation of something that either the protago-

nist did or didn't know. The resolution is the outcome of the story. Does the protagonist meet his/her goal? Does it still matter? Did the goal change for the better or for the worse? JOSH

artwork

Artwork is a publishing term meaning text and/or material prepared for reproduction and included in a book. PANDORA

asterisk (*) [See also Dinkus/Footnote/Drop down]

An asterisk symbol (*) can be used in your novel as a reference mark. It's placed at the end of a phrase or sentence that is being noted, and at the beginning of the linked footnote or endnote at the bottom of the page or end of the book. In the past, asterisks were used to show items in a list when people used typewriters instead of computers. Asterisks grouped together are sometimes used in novels to indicate a change of theme, time, place, or thought. However, it's now common to leave a double-space blank in a novel. Asterisks were also used to indicate the omission of letters in words readers could find offensive. For example: That was a f***in' stupid thing to say. Today many publishers and writers spell out the words. VIOLET

attributions [See also Dialogue/Quotation marks/Speech marks]

Attributions are words used to show how characters are acting or feeling when they are speaking, and who is speaking. For example: She pleaded. Josh said. BIANCA

audience [See also Metaphor]

Audience can be a metaphor for your readers. Imagine your novel is a play with actors, a setting, and action divided into scenes. Your readers are the audience. Keep your audience constantly in mind when you're writing your novel. DAPHNE

audio books

Audio books—reading-with-your-ears format—are fantastic for visually disabled readers and are a growing popular format. Audio books tap in to a busy reader's need for a convenient way to support active lifestyles. Any fictional genre makes an excellent audio book because of the storytelling aspect. Technology is helping the listening-to-books industry to expand. JOSH

> *Playing audio books of popular fiction can kill the time for long-haul car or truck journeys.*

author bio [See also Pen Name/Prelims]

An author bio is a short snatch of information (about 50–100 words) about you—the author. Check out other authors' bios. Paperback novels usually have a paragraph or two about the author on an early inside page. Hardback novels have author detail on the inside back flap of the dust jacket. List your most impressive or most recent relevant accomplishments. You can also write your bio with a quirky light touch. Keep your author bio on hand when you're preparing your manuscript for publication. If you're using a pen name you can go to town creating an engaging fictional bio. GINA

> *Keep it short. Watch your bio doesn't become OTT.*

author platform [See also Online presence]

An author platform refers to the writer's reach and includes social media such as websites and blogs, speaking engagements, workshop presentations, mailing lists and other ways the author communicates with potential book buyers. Mainstream publishers will be interested in an author's novel if the author has a big or reasonable platform. They will want to know how the author's platform will sell books. Obviously if you're self-publishing and want reasonable sales you'll need to work on building an author platform. Your sales and marketing will hinge on your platform. PANDORA

Your author platform is equally important no matter which publishing path you choose.

author's corrections [See also Editing]

Author's corrections is a phrase used by editors and publishers to refer to corrections an author has made to their novel during the publishing process. BILL

Be flexible. Negotiate with editors and publishers. They will be working with you, the author, to produce the best novel possible.

B

back cover copy [See also Blurb/e-book/Panel copy]

Back cover copy, aka blurb, is important to sell your novel. The amount of input you have into your back-cover copy in a traditional, small or independent publishing house can vary. A cover copywriter may be assigned to your novel or your editor may have input into writing your back-cover copy. BILL

If you're into DIY publishing you'll have to write your own back-cover copy for your print or e-book.

back matter [See also Acknowledgements/Dedication/Front matter]

Back matter—sometimes called *end matter* and *endnotes*—refers to the pages after the main text at the back of your novel. Back matter can include an index, bibliographies, appendices, lengthy dedications, acknowledgements, information about the author, author's notes, book club notes, sample chapters of another novel by the author, advertisements for other novels by the same author, or novels in the same genre and published by the same publisher. BILL

backstory [See also Flashback/Pandora's Box/Transitions]

Backstory is what happened to your characters before Page One. It can be like a Pandora's Box that holds your characters' pasts and motivations. You can write backstory as flashbacks but watch you don't bore or confuse your readers when you are introducing flashbacks into your novel. BILL

Don't overdo backstory, also known as info dumping. It can slow your plot. Drip feed or add snippets.

back up [See also Cloud/DIY Cloud/External storage device/USB]

Back up and store your work in as many different ways as possible. Always have a backup plan. There are endless sad stories about novelists literally losing their plots. They've left their novels in buses, taxis, trains, ferries and planes. Novels (hidden inside laptops) have been stolen—never to see daylight again. Or a computer crashes and so has the novel. A happier outcome to these tragic tales of print and electronic loss is to have a backup plan which involves multiple backups. If you've started a novel—planning to write 800+ pages (estimating it will take four or five years before it's published and wins the Man Booker prize)—a backup plan is essential. Your plan can include using your brain, and pen and paper although these last two are definitely not reliable, CDs, DVDs, USB flash drives, external storage devices and online backups are options that work well. JOSH

One of our members knows a successful novelist who kept the hard copy of his novel safe and sound in the freezer section of his fridge. The house burnt down but his novel was safe!

bad writing days

Bad writing days happen. Don't beat yourself up if you have a bad writing day. Accept king-hits from life events. Allow yourself guilt-free space. DAPHNE

beginning

Beginning your novel is a buzz. Savour the euphoria. Every writer has a different mindset, writing routine and process they use to continue writing their novel once they have started. There are no rules to follow. Just write! DAPHNE

Don't write for the money. There isn't any to begin with. Write because you want to write a novel.

bestseller

A bestseller, sometimes called a blockbuster novel, is a novel noted for the speed and volume of its sales. Hype—high-pressure advertising and social media tie-ins—can increase total volume and single-title sales. However, the book trade cannot guarantee hype will make a novel Number One on the Bestseller list. The earliest recorded use of the term bestseller was in 1902. After many rejections, *Gone with the Wind* (1936) became a bestseller clocking up 3.5 million sales in 9 years—helped by the MGM film and actor Clarke Gable who starred in the film. In 2003-6 Dan Brown's novel, *The Da Vinci Code*, sold eight million copies—outselling every previous bestseller—and faster. Jeffrey Archer, one of the most successful writers in the world has sales of his novels around 330 million. Some self-published authors have written e-books that have become unbelievably successful bestsellers. A novel can become a bestseller posthumously. This could be really annoying for the author—if the author was still alive. BIANCA

Take heart! Many novels have jumped from obscurity to the top of the bestseller list several years after they're published or snatched from on-line publishing lists to become massive bestsellers.

beta readers [See also Track Changes]

Beta readers are the important first readers of your completed novel. You need the magical number of three readers willing to test read your manuscript. Too many critics or too much feedback and you won't know what to do with it. Choose readers that are empathetic to the genre of your type of writing i.e. crime fiction. Present your manuscript in the form that is easiest for them to read i.e. hard copy so they can add their written suggestions, or digital so they can use Track Changes to offer their suggestions. Give your beta readers a deadline of 2-3 weeks and tell them what you want to achieve. For instance: Do they think your story is believable? Does your novel have plot holes? Do parts need clarifying? Is the ending satisfying? Can they think of anything to improve your novel? Request them to mark where they stop as they read throughout your novel. This may alert you to gaps in your plot. GINA

Writing groups are excellent sources to find beta readers.

between/among

Between and Among are two words that can confuse writers. Between comes from an Old English word betweonum meaning *by two each.* It was eventually shortened to *between.* Use *between* to discuss two things. Among comes from an Old English word *on-gemang* meaning *in a crowd.* It was eventually shortened to *among.* Use *among* to discuss three or more things. DIGBY

the Big Five publishers [See also The Big Six publishers]

The Big Five publishers were once the Big Six mainstream or traditional publishers. LEE

When you submit your novel to a mainstream publisher check they haven't merged.

the Big Six publishers [See also DIY publishing/Mainstream publishing]

The Big Six publishers (Random House, HarperCollins, Penguin Group, Macmillan, Simon & Schuster and Hachette Book Group) were the gatekeepers to a novel's success only a few years ago. Now they have morphed into the Big Five. LEE

When you submit your novel to a mainstream publisher check they are still working independently.

the Black Hole [See also 30,000 words]

The Black Hole is a writerly term to describe when a writer gets stuck. It's not as drastic as writers' block and successful and prolific authors—even famous—have an issue with the black hole at some time. It usually happens at the 30,000-word or 200-page mark. There are many solutions such as going back to where you were happy with your novel. Don't be afraid to delete thousands of words, or numbers of pages in order to give yourself a place where you can drive your novel forward. Note: don't forget to keep a separate dump file for the text you delete. Writers who plan in great detail, or at least have some idea of the ending, rarely have an issue with the black hole. DAPHNE

If you're really stuck, put your novel away for a while and begin something else. Don't panic. Amazing as it seems a story can keep developing in the subconscious mind.

bleed

Bleed is a printing and design term to refer to the part of an image, illustration or print that runs past the usual margins to the edge of the page. VIOLET

body [See also Self-publishing/Typeface]

Body is a design term that refers to the main text of the book. If you are self-publishing and using interior page-design software or you have hired a book designer, readability of the text is vital. VIOLET

blog [See also Blog author tours/Blogging/Social media]

A blog, shortened from *web log*, is an online diary you can update regularly—an immediate journal-slash-diary. Your website can incorporate a blog. Your blog's content can include online videos, photos and links to other sites with space for on-screen readers' posts (comments). One or more people can manage a blog, with regular entries or posts, or you can guest on another blogger's blog. A blog can be an excellent marketing tool for a novelist. You can give readers news about your books, author events, or you can tempt them into buying your book by posting the first or many chapters. Check out other writers' blogs in the blogosphere. PANDORA

> *Don't share stuff on a blog you'll regret later. The same laws and restrictions apply on screen as to what you write on a page.*

blog author tours

Blog author tours (virtual author tours) may be organised by your publisher, or you can work with a team of writerly colleagues and organise you own virtual author tours for promotion. PANDORA

blogging

Blogging is when you write daily, weekly, or monthly posts on your blog or on someone else's blog. A blog can have value as a marketing tool in selling your novel. Beware—it's time consuming. Some publishers and editors may recognise your blogging skills make you more marketable as an author. PANDORA

If blogging is not your thing don't bother. Keep writing your novel.

blue pen [See also Red pen/Proofreading]

A blue pen is traditionally used by editors to make corrections. Queries are written in blue pen on a manuscript. These queries should be finalised before the typesetting process of your novel. Corrections are written above the line, and the margins are used for writing heading codes, figure numbers, queries or special instructions to the designers. VIOLET

Track Changes (an advanced feature in Microsoft Word) is commonly used today to edit your novel digitally.

blurb [See also Elevator pitch/Book description /Panel copy]

The blurb is a sales hook to bring on a book-buying impulse. Blurbs are short, give an idea of what the novel is about, but they don't give away the ending. It is usually found on the back cover of paperback books. On hard covered books the blurb can be found on the back cover, inside the front cover, or on the flap of a novel's dust jacket to promote the novel. In 1907, American author and cartoonist, Gelett Burgess, was a guest speaker at a booksellers' convention. He made hundreds of fake covers (featuring a very attractive woman Miss Belinda Blurb) and wrote the back-cover text to pitch his new book. After this time the term blurb was used to describe text to promote a book.

Practice writing the blurb for your novel in 25, 50, 100, and 150 words. When you pitch your novel you can use any of these blurbs.

blurbing [See also Strapline]

Blurbing, or an endorsement on a novel's front or back cover, is a short favourable comment acknowledged by the writer of the blurbing. For example: *A marvellous novel! C. Dickens.* Blurbing works as a small advertisement telling browsers and would-be buyers your novel is worth buying and reading. It also works as a small advertisement for the writer of the blurbing—the blurbee. Blurbings are usually organised through publishers i.e. they find the celebs or best-selling authors to be blurbees. You can organise your own blurbing if you are a DIY author. PANDORA

When you become a successful author be prepared to be a blurbee.

book block [See also Case/Casebound]

Book block is a traditional publishing term for the bound sections of your print novel before it is inserted into the cover. VIOLET

book club

A book club is where book-loving members meet to have fun and discuss books they've read. Joining a book club can assist would-be novel writers. It's good to read novels by other authors and to discover how readers interpret them. DAPHNE

book deal [See also Contract/Indie publishers]

A book deal is negotiations between you, the Writer (the Party of the First Part) submitting it to the Publisher (the Party of the Second Part) for consideration. This might involve a Party of the Third Part (a literary agent) but not always. The whole process can take weeks, months, or even longer before a book deal is done. LEE

If you don't have an agent we suggest you join a recognised Authors' Society to assist you in negotiating the legal complexities of a book deal with mainstream publishers.

book description [See also Elevator pitch/Pitch]

A book description is an overview of your novel—without an ending—and is needed to market your book. If you've signed with a mainstream publisher you may be working with an editor to produce your book description for an e-book edition. If you plan to sign with an independent (Indie), or small-press publisher, or self-publish, you will need a book description. If you self-publish, your online book description is what will sell your novel directly to the reader. In your book description you will need to include elements such as the main characters, plot, tone, genre and comparable titles. VIOLET

Write about your novel in a compelling fashion, but don't go in to much detail with the plot and don't reveal your ending.

book design [See also Cover design/Prelims]

A book design for print books has traditional elements to assist the reader to navigate through the pages. The cover, prelim and end pages, contribute to a traditional book design.

A print book design uses the symmetry of the two-page spread as the basis of the design with layouts that include running heads and/or footers, margins, and page numbers. The text is usually divided in chapters with artwork to link the theme of the book. JOSH

If your novel is published by traditional or independent publishers the design of your novel will be in professional hands with little or no input from you. If you are self-publishing you will be making the decisions.

book design package

[See also Book designer/Cover design/Self-publishing]

A book design package is a package you can buy at a reasonable cost from websites such as 99designs and Fiverr.com if you are self-publishing. The package can include the cover design and layout of your novel. LEE

Take note that lower-cost design packages (even if the cover designs are sold as one-offs) won't include exclusivity on stock images. Your cover photo could pop up on other books.

book designer [See also Cover design/Self-publishing]

A book designer is a graphic designer who specialises in designing covers and layouts for books. You can hire a freelance book designer directly to design your book. It is an expensive option if you are self-publishing but the results can be stunning. Most designers will chat or email with you about the themes and tone of your novel and set up a budget and timeline. DIGBY

Contracts should spell out revisions and changes allowed and deadlines for delivering proposal sketches, first drafts and revisions. If you're going to be difficult and want a lot of changes and requests you will be paying for them.

book launch [See also Book signing/Marketing/Talks]

A book launch is an event when your novel is launched (presented) to the public. It's an excellent opportunity to market and sell copies of your novel. If you are a best-selling author your publisher *may* fund and organise your book launch, hopefully arrange an upmarket location, and food and drinks for the guests. As the author you will be required to make a short speech and sign copies of your novel, which will be for sale. Don't forget to thank everyone connected with the writing and publishing of your novel. If you're a mid-list author or self-publishing your novel, you'll need to plan your own book launch. Think local. The nearest friendly library or bookshop will make an excellent venue and you can self-cater to provide tea and coffee or a glass of wine and nibbles of some sort. **PANDORA**

Be prepared to read aloud an entertaining or emotional few pages from your novel. Use post-it flags to mark pages when you do a reading at your book launch, interview or talks.

book signing [See also Interviews/Marketing/Talks]

Book signing is when you write your signature, and sometimes a catchy, or edgy few words inside your novel for the buyer e.g. *For Xanthe ... Happy Divorce!* Book signings usually occur at bookshops, writers' festivals, et cetera. It's an excellent way to meet your readers and increase sales of your novel.

When you sign your novel it personalises the experience for the book-buyer or reader. The title page of a book is traditionally reserved for a book's author to sign. HarperCollins US has joined forces with a company called Autography, developing a technology that allows the virtual signing of e-books. The signed page can include a photograph of the reader with the author of the augmented book. GINA

When you sign a book make sure you use the correct spelling for the book-buyer's name or the person who's receiving your book as a gift.

book summary [See Book description]

book tour [See also Blog author tours/Interviews]

A book tour is a promotional and marketing tool. Once it was accepted an author would tour, sometimes with other authors or literary board members, with funding from your publisher or a literary board, to promote your novel at libraries, bookstores and events. If you're a DIY published author you can organise your own real-time or online book tour—with or without writerly colleagues. GINA

book trailer [See also Social media/Video trailer]

A book trailer is a short video or movie to promote a book. Book trailers are usually viewed using electronic devices. A book trailer takes quite a degree of skill and expertise to produce and if you employ professionals it can be quite expensive. JOSH

A book trailer may be all you need to make your novel a bestseller.

bought/brought [See also Tense/Verb]

Bought and *brought* can be confusing words for writers. *Bought* is the past tense of *to buy*. For example: Gina bought bones for the dog. *Brought* is the past tense of the verb *to bring*. For example: Daphne brought her husband's parsnip wine to the writers group meeting. GINA

Connect the letter r in bring, with the letter r in brought.

brackets () [] {} // [See also Comma/Dash]

There are four kinds of brackets (also called parentheses). Round brackets ( ) are most commonly used. They are used to enclose text that provides additional information. When you enclose text in brackets, punctuation in the sentence stays the same. Square brackets [ ] are used to enclose material that was not written by the author of the sentence. Square brackets are also used for explanations within direct quotations, and editorial comments or queries. Curly brackets { } brackets are mostly used in mathematics, and as a design feature. Slash brackets // enclose letters that represent a sound. For example: the /oo/ sound in *book*. They are also used for dates written in numerals. 24/7/09. DIGBY

You can use commas or dashes as an alternative to brackets to enclose additional information in a sentence.

brainstorming [See also Idea/Mind mapping]

Brainstorming is a way to come up with ideas for your present or next novel. It's an excellent strategy to use to overcome a problem or a brick-wall issue in your writing. Brainstorm everything you can think of about your writing or an issue on a page. BIANCA

Do not throw away one single idea. Keep an Ideas file on a card system, in a notebook, or as a computer file.

branding [See also F2F /Marketing/Pen name]

Branding is important in the publishing world. If a mainstream publisher publishes your novel, they'll make decisions on your behalf—how you and your books are marketed and/or branded. If you're self-publishing you'll need to do all the work. First you'll need to indicate the genre of your novel (e.g. historical thriller) then aim for a consistent message around you and your writing. Think about how you will market yourself: personal appearances, use of social media including email, a website, Facebook, Twitter et cetera and the core values you want to get across. Some introverted authors find it's comforting to imagine they're a persona they can hang in a wardrobe and retrieve for personal appearances and interviews. Comfortingly, most would-be book-buyers don't choose a book by its publisher. Buyers look for a great entertaining read, genre, or an author when they buy a book. Or they may buy your novel because of its cover! BIANCA

The term branding comes from the branding of cattle with a specific mark to identify the owner. Obviously this does not apply to writers.

browsing [See also Blurb/Opening sentence/Title]

Browsing translates as mooching around books' in real-time or online. As a writer, it's a serendipitous way of researching, estimating your novel's chances in the current market or checking the sale of your novel. You can read the back cover copy, online descriptions or first lines of novels, and you can read the last lines to see if the butler did it. Sadly many chain bookstores have closed so you will have to go on the hunt for small independent bookshops.

Look for a bookstore with staff that remembers what you like and can recommend new books for you. Chat to the staff to find out who is writing what. What are mainstream publishers publishing and who are they publishing? Browse online. What titles, authors and genres are online bestsellers? Check thumbprint-size covers online, read the titles, and the book descriptions. GINA

Vintage book-selling know-how: it takes a would-be buyer eight seconds to read a title and fifteen seconds to read the back cover blurb. Then they may consider buying your novel!

bullets [See also Lists]

Bullets—also called bullet points and dot points—are punctuation marks used to list items in a text. Asterisks frequently took the place of bullets in the days before computers. Once computers and word processors became common, people could create lists easily using bullet points. Bullets were originally called dot points, but the black dots reminded people of bullet holes. Today bullet points are referred to simply as bullets. DIGBY

the business of writing [See also Income]

The business of writing is managing and earning money from your writing. If you earn money from your writing you become a sole trader or small business according to taxation departments. Wear two hats when you write a novel; one for writing, one for business. When you wear your business hat keep an account of the cash in/cash out connected with your writing. Consider whether you need a tax agent, an accountant, a computer-accounting program, a company structure, a literary agent, a speakers' agency to handle your appearance bookings, and a publicist to handle your image as an author. Obviously these business services are costly but it's important to keep them in mind when you become a successful novelist. Acquiring a business card and letterhead are inexpensive ways to project your brand as a novelist. Set up rigorous records e.g. the date, publisher and address when you submit your novel to a mainstream or Indie publisher and detailed records of your DIY publishing. PANDORA

As a sole trader, ensure you block breaks for a vacation in your diary—even a staycation. You need to have holidays—whether you write during them or not!

but [See also And/Conjunction/Transitions]

But is a connecting word—a conjunction. In the past it was frowned upon to begin a sentence with but—today it's acceptable. But is also an excellent transition word. DIGBY

C

café writing [See also Listening/Notebook/Writers' Groups]

Café writing has been made famous by single mum, JK Rowling, who wrote a series of best-selling books about a boy wizard. Tapping away on a laptop or scribbling in a notebook amongst the bustle and chatter of a café or coffee shop may work for you. JK Rowling wrote nine books in ten years. Not all were written in cafes and she did receive eleven rejections before she was first published. Many cafes are happy to have a writer-in-residence working at a window table, or a writers' group meeting in café—it's good for the trade. LEE

When you visit a café bring your notebook, laptop or device. Watch, listen and note the passing parade.

café rules for writers [See also Listening/Notebook/Writers' Groups]

Make sure you order at least one drink each hour. Choose a small table. Use battery power so you don't have power leads snaking across the café. Mute the sound on your device or laptop. Don't hog bandwidth by downloading large files and leave a tip. BILL

Look for cafes with Free Wi-Fi *and follow café rules for writers so you're always welcome at your local café.*

Camp NaNoWriMo [See also NaNoWriMo]

Camp NaNoWriMo is a virtual camp—*a literary adventure* for writers held in April and July by *Berkeley's Office of Letters and Lights*, the same non-profit organisation that sponsors November's national novel writing month. Camp NaNoWriMo is low-key and fun with posts of camp songs, cabin mates, survival kits et cetera and has attracted more than 200,000 participants in the past.

Campers can write on a computer, by hand or on a smart phone. They don't have to meet the November event's 50,000-word goal and they aren't limited to writing a novel. They can take on whatever project they choose. Participants have worked in a variety of genres including screenplay, non-fiction, and short stories. JOSH

camera-ready copy

Camera-ready copy (CRC) is a printing and publishing term for copy that is ready for the printer to use for making a printing plate. VIOLET

canon

A canon in the literary sense (not the battle weapon) refers to a group of works by an author or authors who are accepted as authorities in their fields and their writings are seen to constitute a serious body of literature. JOSH

> *A popular literary cannon could include: Pride and Prejudice, To Kill a Mockingbird, Jane Eyre, The Great Gatsby, A Tale of Two Cities et cetera.*

capital letters [See also Lower case lettering/Upper case lettering]

Capital letters are always used to start a sentence. They are also used for proper nouns and acronyms. Use capital Letters in the Text of your Novel with Caution. JOSH

Publishers have a house style for the use of initial caps—capital letters.

CC [See also Email]

Cc is an abbreviation of the words *carbon copy*. Inked paper (carbon paper) was used in the past to create copies of writing. Cc is used to indicate the message has been sent to people in the Cc address line of an email. DIGBY

Always edit your emails before you send them. Check and recheck the address line.

caret [See also Mark-ups]

Caret (not to be confused with a measurement of diamonds) is the editing term for an insertion mark on copy. BIANCA

case [See also Hardback/Paperback]

Case is a printing term for the assembled front, back and spine-covering material into which the book block (the text of your novel) is bound. VIOLET

casebound

This is the technical term for the hardback or hardcover book. VIOLET

category [See Genre]

celebrity author [See also Marketing]

A celebrity author is either a celebrity who has written a novel, or a person who has become a celebrity because of writing one or many novels and has gained mega sales. Celebrity authors usually go through the publicity machine and come out the other end as a *must have* speaker at writers' festivals et cetera. They usually have up-market book signings and are always available for photos, interviews, as writers of articles about writing—particular their novel(s)—supplier of *free* quotes by accepting multi-media appearances. A celebrity author's readers morph into fans. VIOLET

Success can get in the way if you want time to write a novel!

chapter [See also Cliff-hanger/Scene]

A chapter is a division of text within your novel. It's a way to collect scenes, to group them together for your story arc. Chapters can be numbered or titled. Compare the number and word-lengths of chapters in similar novels written in your genre. Consider finishing chapters with cliff-hangers—hooks to keep the reader reading. You can start a new chapter to give your reader a break from the tension of the plot, to show the passing of time, when you're changing narrators or a point-of-view, to increase the tension or when you've completed a scene or scenes. LEE

chapter outline [See also Scene]

A chapter outline is a quick summary of the key elements in a chapter. It's a tool you can use when you're writing your novel. It can help you find potholes in your plot, keep track of character development, et cetera in your writing process. Questions to ask yourself as you write the outline: What is happening in this chapter? How does it alter my character(s)? How does it offer some new perception for my reader? BILL

Many publishers require a chapter outline when you submit your novel.

chapter summary [See also POV]

A chapter summary is equivalent to a chapter outline, only it's written *after* the first draft is completed. It's an excellent tool to use when you're editing completed drafts of your novel. It gives you a 360-degree view of your novel and captures core elements of your plot and characters. It will also reveal gaps in your writing, e.g. gaps in the plot, missing information, excess backstory, faulty point-of-views, et cetera. Set up a structure to suit the writing style of your novel with headings such as chapter, page number, POV (point-of-view), setting, character(s), time, season, year, place, action, and research needed. GINA

character arc

[See also Character-driven novel/Character profiles/Characters]

A character arc is formed from entrances and exits of a character in your novel. When you're rewriting it's handy to keep track of character arcs in case you need to delete or enlarge—maybe combine characters in your novel. The word *arc* can also refer to the growth or development of your character through your novel. JOSH

character-driven novel

[See also Character arc/Character profiles/Characters]

A character-driven novel is one where a character's decisions and actions develop and drive the plot of a novel. VIOLET

It's worth taking the time to work out what makes your characters tick. Then you can create believable characters.

character profiles [See also Character arc/Character-driven novel]

Character profiles can be brief, bullet-point info, or one page or longer descriptions of your characters. Describe your characters—eye and hair colour, height, clothes, pets, likes and dislikes et cetera. You can also write detailed descriptions to include your character's physicality, psychological profile, and family history. Character profiles are useful, especially when you're beginning your novel. GINA

Character profiles are useful when you forget a character's name or the colour of their eyes.

characters [See also Antagonist/Helper/Protagonist]

Characters are a vital element in a novel. Characters can be people, vampires, ghosts, aliens, time-travellers, wizards, elves, animals—whatever. You need main characters and minor characters for your novel. For a basic novel you need to fill the three main character roles: Protagonist, Antagonist and Helper. To support the three you need six or more minor characters, and a big or small cast of walk-on characters. Characters are often referred to as two, three or four-dimensional characters. Four-dimensional characters are supposed to leap off the page. You don't want characters referred to as cardboard, tissue paper or nano-thin. BILL

Two-dimensional characters can work in a novel if you're writing a page-turning action plot.

Chekov's rifle

Chekov's rifle is an effective plot device. The phrase comes from a quote by Anton Chekhov. *One must not put a loaded rifle on the stage if no one is thinking of firing it.* Translated: Keep a close watch on any object e.g. a gun, or a skill such as crack-shooting acquired by your protagonist in scenes or chapters. Does your character use the object or skill later? If not delete the references from your text. LEE

chick-lit [See also Cover design/Hen-lit/Romantic fiction]

Chick-lit—also spelt *chic-lit*—is a term to describe popular novels written for women under 30. They are novels filled with young, attractive characters, romance, friendships, clothes and shoes. They make great sexy, fun reads and sell well. BIANCA

There's a misconception that writing chick-lit is easy. Wrong! Writing chick-lit is hard work and the novels often contain helpful life-messages.

choosing a pen name [See also Anon/Marketing]

There are unlimited reasons for choosing a pen name, or names. You can choose a genderless name, e.g. JK Rowling or an alphabetical strategic name e.g. a surname beginning with early alphabet initials so the novels are quickly located on a bookshelf. Maybe you'll have several pen names? Perhaps you can't stand your name and want to change it? Or you may choose a pen name that matches the genre in which you write. You can write contemporary fiction under one name, romance under another and choose another name when you write crime and erotic fiction. If you're a writer of prize-winning literary novels you could decide to write—equally well-crafted—crime fiction novels in order to pay the bills. Watch out your name doesn't date or age you if you're writing Young Adult novels. Choose a modern name and find a younger photograph of yourself to use for publicity. Best-selling authors have been known to use a pen name to check their novel's saleability. This is not easy to do in our techno-savvy world where you can be outed, e.g. JK Rowling when she wrote her first crime fiction. However, Agatha Christie wrote love stories under the pseudonym of Mary Westmacott and all concerned were sworn to secrecy. VIOLET

Beware of signing the wrong name at book signings.

chronological order [See also Back matter/Historical fiction]

Chronological order—an organised sequence of timed events —is a useful structure to build a novel. A novel can also have a *chronology of events* at the end of the book, which is helpful for readers if you're writing historical fiction. DAPHNE

clause [See also Grammar/Subject/Verb]

A clause is a grammatical term to describe a group of related words that contain a subject and a verb. Clauses can be independent and stand alone as a sentence, and dependent when they cannot stand alone as a sentence. An independent clause and a dependent clause can be used together to make a sentence. For example: When she turned over a new leaf we found we were on the same page. DIGBY

clean copy

Clean copy is a writerly term that implies the hard or digital copy you present to an agent or publisher is formatted and edited well. This is the first step in getting your novel published. **BILL**

cliché [See also Figure of speech/Metaphor/Simile]

A cliché is a well-known expression that has been used so often it no longer carries as much meaning or excitement as it did originally. For example: lost the plot, by the book, turning over a new leaf, leaping off the page, on the same page. Clichés in writing are equal to signs you see everywhere such as a dog with a slash through it to indicate *no dogs allowed*. It's up to the novelist to hit readers with original clichés. **BIANCA**

Clichés such as drop-dead gorgeous *and* fairy-tale wedding *still work well in romantic novels.*

cliff-hanger [See also Chapter/Dialogue/Suspense]

A cliff-hanger is a term for a technique using dialogue or action that causes suspense. It is a useful technique to use at the end of a chapter—holding back the consequence of an action or dialogue until the next chapter. **LEE**

cloud [See also Backup/DIY Cloud]

Cloud is a cyberspace storage supplier of choice. An amount of storage is free, and after that you need to subscribe. **JOSH**

CMYK

CMYK is an abbreviation for the printing term cyan, magenta, black and yellow. The four colours used in print. **VIOLET**

colloquial language [See also Dialogue/Language]

Colloquial language is an informal, conversational style of speech. It is commonly used in contemporary novels. **BILL**

colon (:) [See also Dash/Punctuation]

A colon (:) is a punctuation mark. It was originally used to mean *take a long pause. Colon* is Greek for *limb* or the verse of a poem.

The colon has many uses, such as to introduce a list, and to give more details about something that has been said in a sentence. For example: There are two main groups of novels: literary and popular. Some novelists ignore the colon completely and use a dash. As long as your publisher approves the use of a colon it's cool. **BILL**

comma (,) [See also Colon/Semicolon/ Serial comma]

A comma (,) is a punctuation mark. It was originally used to mean *take a short pause. Comma* is Greek for *cutting off.*

A comma's main function is to avoid confusion when you are reading—to make the meaning clearer. Use a comma to prevent ambiguity. For example: We are going to eat Lewis before we go out. We are going to eat, Lewis, before we go out.

You can also use a comma to separate a list of adjectives, and a string of nouns. For example: A novel needs characters, setting, and a plot. A comma is used to mark off a statement, which is an aside from the main sentence. For example: The local bus, driven by Alf, screamed to a halt outside the bookshop. **DIGBY**

Don't scatter commas like confetti. The modern trend is to use commas sparingly. When in doubt, leave them out.

comma splice [See also Comma/Punctuation/Semicolon]

A comma splice occurs when a comma is used to join two independent clauses (e.g. I've been so busy, I haven't touched my novel.) Removing the comma doesn't correct the splice but turns it into a run-on sentence. To correct a comma splice use a semi-colon, dash or period (i.e. make the two clauses separate sentences) or use a coordinating conjunction to follow the comma. For example: I've been so busy; I haven't touched my novel. Or, I've been so busy and I haven't touched my novel. JOSH

commercial fiction [See also Genre/Literary novels]

Commercial fiction is a term for novels that are as well written as literary novels but in a different way. Commercial novels are usually genre specific i.e. they fit into categories such as crime, sci-fi, and romantic fiction et cetera. However, many commercial novels cross over between the literary and contemporary-fiction divide. They are usually fast-paced and have a strong plot line with engaging characters. Publishers expect to make a profit from commercial, contemporary and genre novels because they have a larger buyer market than literary novels. BILL

comparable comps titles [See also Query]

Comparable comps titles is a phrase to describe comparing similar published novels in competition with yours. It can make a writer feel squeamish and embarrassed comparing their novel with bestsellers and greats but it's essential in marketing your novel. When you compare your novel with a similar published novel it gives the agent, publisher and onscreen reader a frame of reference. VIOLET

Watch you don't go OTT in choosing amazingly successful novels to compare with yours!

competitions

Competitions with prizes where you can win a publishing contract for your unpublished novel, or an award for a published novel can make a great impact on an author's career. Always check and double-check the rules and guidelines. If you've already written a published novel your publisher may submit it or you can submit it. Check submission details. They're always subject to change. BILL

Edit your entry thoroughly.

complex sentence [See also Clause/Compound sentence/Sentence]

A complex sentence is made of a dependent clause and an independent clause. For example: Although the dog was well trained, he refused to perform tricks. GINA

compound sentence [See also Clause/Complex sentence/Sentence]

A compound sentence is made of two dependent clauses. A semi-colon (;) is used to join them. For example: It was a kernel of an idea; an idea he could use to start his novel. GINA

computer graphics [See also Graphic novel]

Computer graphics are pictorial or diagrammatic images displayed on a computer and created by means of a keyboard, a mouse or light pen. JOSH

concrete noun [See also Abstract noun/Grammar/Noun]

A concrete noun is the name of a thing that can be seen or touched. Concrete nouns help writers create real worlds. DIGBY

conjunction [See also And/But/Grammar]

A conjunction is a word that connects or links other words in sentences. For example: such, as, and, but, or, nor, since, unless, however—et cetera. DIGBY

Watch your use of conjunctions if you're writing an action novel. You don't want too many long sentences.

contemporary fiction [See Commercial fiction]

content editing [See Copy editing/Proofreading/Structural editor]

content maker [See also Marketing/Marketing tools]

Content maker is a modern term for a writer who writes online articles, blogs and posts et cetera for social media platforms. LEE

Be on the lookout for any opportunities to write content that will promote your novel.

contract [See also Agent/Deadline/Publishers]

A contract is a legal document. Societies and organisations for authors and writers run contract advisory services for a small fee. Most publishers will offer an acceptable contract but you can't depend on your publisher being in the *most* group. BILL

contraction [See also Apostrophe/Dialogue/Phrase]

A contraction is a shortened word or phrase. When you use contractions in your writing, such as in dialogue, it makes the dialogue seem more natural. There are two types of contraction—single words and phrases. Single words can become contractions when the middle letters are left out. For example: Dr is a contraction of Doctor. Phrases can become contractions when letters are left out, and the words become one word. An apostrophe is used to show letters have been left out. For example: Don't is a contraction of do not. Haven't is a contraction of have not. DIGBY

copy

Copy is a publishing term used for manuscript pages before they are set in type. VIOLET

copy editing [See also Proofreading/Structural editor]

Copy editing is essential to prepare a manuscript for typesetting and publishing. A mainstream publisher will employ a copy editor who will work with an author to prepare their manuscript. If you're self-publishing you will need to do your own copy editing or employ a copy editor. VIOLET

> *Members highly recommend employing a copy editor if you are self-publishing. Copy editors are worth their weight in gold!*

copy editor [See also Defamation/Proofreading/structural editor]

A copy editor works with the author to improve clarity and consistency of content and style. They correct typos, spelling, punctuation, and grammar. A copy editor will also check for defamation in your text, and if you're traditionally published they will ensure the house style has been correctly implemented. The format and style of the manuscript is standardised by the copy editor for the typesetter. Specific fonts for chapter headings, text and paragraph indentations and chapter divisions will be formatted. If there are fragments of text that stand out such as emails they will require a different font. BILL

copyright (©) [See also Contract/Plagiarism]

Copyright (©) is established automatically on creation of your novel. It gives legal protection to writers against the unauthorised copying of their work. The writer(s), or the person who commissioned the work—subject to an alternative agreement—owns copyright. In Australia, US and UK, copyright remains for 70 years after the death of the author and until that point permission should be requested to use or quote from works. PANDORA

> © only protects the expression of your idea. You cannot copyright the idea itself.

cosy crime fiction [See also The Golden Age/Series]

Cosy crime fiction is a writerly term for a murder mystery without the gore. Unlike cosy crime fiction in the 1920s and 30s, today's cosy crime fiction novels have characters, relevant themes and real-time experiences to attract a modern audience of readers. VIOLET

> Cosy crime fiction is an excellent genre if you want to write novels that will develop into a series.

cover design [See also Book design/Book design package/Self-publishing]

The cover design of a novel has a huge impact on sales. Most readers ignore the adage, *Don't judge a book by its cover* and will buy your book by the cover. As well as a great title, a successful cover design can capture the message of your novel in an image. The wrong cover design can add to misinterpretation of the novel inside the cover, for example: a light, fun cover with glittery fonts can indicate a romance. Blood red or black fonts on a murky background can indicate crime fiction. Swap the covers on the novels and readers will not be happy. Most novelists published by mainstream publishers are not consulted about their cover design. You have to trust your publisher knows which cover designs are hot, or cool for your intended readers and will sell novels. If you are self-publishing you can buy a book design package that includes a cover design or have your self-publishing service do the cover design. A budget option is to design your own cover using book design templates and purchase fonts or stock photography. LEE

Whatever path you take your cover must stand out, and be on-trend—all in a thumbprint-size image to stand out on a screen.

cover letter [See also QL/Query/Online slush pile]

A cover letter (also called a QL or query letter) can be your one and only chance to keep your novel out of the slush pile. Many agents or publishers only require a cover or a query email from an author. Your cover letter, or query, should contain a brief summary of your novel, why it's special, why it suits the agent's or publisher's list. Include a brief summary of your writing credits and mention writing courses, membership of any professional writing groups, your interest in a genre, or a particular imprint. It can pay to mention professional credits i.e. medical qualifications if you are writing a novel with a medical background. BILL

Obviously if you're self-publishing you won't need a cover letter.

crafting your novel [See also Writing classes and workshops]

Crafting your novel is practising your writing skills and techniques to improve your novel until it's in the best shape it can be. If you work on writing tasks and exercises they will help you to hone your craft. DIGBY

Joining a writing group can help improve your writing skills.

credit-crunch marketing [See also Marketing]

Credit-crunch marketing is a term used at the marketing battlefront. Some publishers are choosing new novels—not so much for their readability—as for their talkability. Publishers are asking questions. Can the author talk to the media? Will the media talk up the novel? Can the novel be talked onto the prize shortlists? Will the novel be talked onto book club lists? And...will the novel be talked about enough so that anyone who buys it will never have to read it? PANDORA

A writer should not be defeated in their quest to write a published novel. It's not difficult to create spin around a well-written novel—a novel that makes a great must-read and brings enjoyment to readers.

crime fiction [See also Cosy Crime fiction/Thrillers/Whodunits]

Crime fiction is a genre of commercial fiction. Within the crime fiction genre there are many subgenres such as cosy crime, psychological mystery, police procedural, detective, thriller and noir thriller. Crime fiction novels require a careful structure since plot is vital. VIOLET

You can break the writer's rule, Write what you know *when you write crime fiction. It's not necessary to be a police constable, lawyer or forensic scientist when you write crime fiction—but it could help.*

crit (critique) groups [See also Feedback]

Crit (critique) groups or clubs are groups of writers who assist and support one another by providing critical comment for members' writing. The crit group can meet face-to-face or online. Caution: a crit group can be tougher than a writers' group. GINA

Watch you're in a crit group that can help rather than hinder your writing. If your crit group isn't working for you hit the road. VIOLET

critical friend [See also Beta reader]

A critical friend is a label for a writerly colleague you trust to give you realistic, valuable feedback about your writing. DAPHNE

A partner, friend or family member may offer to read your work but rarely will they tell you the tough stuff about your writing. They won't want to hurt your feelings.

criticism [See also Editing/Feedback]

Criticism can be positive or negative. Learning to take criticism with a brave face goes with the territory of writing a novel. Instead of seeking approval from friends, family and your writing group ask specific questions such as, *What's wrong with Chapter Seven? How can I make it better?* This is the kind of feedback you need to know as a writer.

Constructive criticism can improve your novel. You can still reject the criticism if you think it's wrong. After you submit your novel to an agent or publisher, they suggest changes you can make to improve it. Accept this criticism, allow it to simmer, and then start revising. DAPHNE

If family, friends or writers' group members nod their heads when you read pages from your novel it's an indication they're too terrified to give you constructive criticism.

cross genre [See also Genre]

Cross genre is when your novel can be linked with two genres for example *historical thriller,* or three genres—*historical noir crime fiction,* or four genres—*paranormal historical noir romance.* VIOLET

crutch words [See also Overused words]

Crutch words such as: then, that, just, very, besides, indeed, of, look, well, and suddenly are unnecessary words. They should be cut when you're self-editing. Cutting your crutch words will tighten your writing. GINA

It will amaze you how easily you can shorten your novel's word count when you cut these words.

cushion deadline [See also Deadline/Contract]

A cushion deadline is an imagined deadline you set yourself—an invented time in which to finish a draft, or editing. Set a realistic deadline for yourself. Write every day to keep your novel in your head. Remember a shark dies if it doesn't keep moving. Set writing goals e.g. write a page a day, 500–1000 words a day, 30 minutes a day or a specific number of scenes or chapters. Add *TK*—an old editing mark meaning 'to come'—in your manuscript to indicate you need to check spelling, a quote or a statistic et cetera later. Agatha Christie set herself three-month deadlines. *Three months seems to me quite a reasonable time to complete a book if one can get right down to it.* Ian Fleming allowed himself a six-week deadline to write a James Bond novel. He broke his writing sessions with time for cocktails and snorkelling in the Caribbean Sea. VIOLET

Some writers discard or ignore deadlines. This is not an advisable attitude if you want to complete your novel.

D

dangling modifier [See also Clause/Participles/Phrase]

A dangling modifier, also called a dangling participle, is a grammatical mistake. It's a word, phrase, or clause that's not placed next to the word it should be modifying or describing. The word, phrase or clause is left dangling! A misplaced or dangling modifier can give the sentence a different meaning and can cause unintentional humour. For example: Smothered in chocolate sauce, Bianca ate the ice cream. BILL

dash (–) [See also Brackets/Em/En]

The dash (–) is used as a punctuation mark. There are two types of dashes: the en-dash and the em-dash. The em-dash is used as a separator, for amplification and to denote abrupt change. Text set apart by dashes stands out more prominently or becomes more emphatic. Commas, brackets and dashes have a similar use and weight in sentences. Use dashes sparingly for the most impact when you write. DIGBY

Visualise your sentence without dashes to see if you have placed them correctly. The sentence should remain grammatical without dashes.

deadline [See also Cushion deadline/The one-point-five rule]

A deadline can be official or soft and cushiony—a deadline you make for yourself. An official deadline with a publishing house is the date agreed to by [you] the author and [editor] when a novel, edited manuscript or proofs are due at the editor's office. Your contract will include a deadline for the delivery of the manuscript of your novel. Be prepared for deadlines. File and/or basket your novel so you can locate it at a minute's notice. Ask for dates when copy edited text or proofs will be sent to you. Make your own soft-cushion (earlier) deadline in case your cat gets run over and you have to take it to the vet or some similar disruption in your life. Estimate how much time you'll need to reach a deadline. Be realistic. There are frequent, very short turn-around times in which to meet deadlines for publishers. VIOLET

Disregard flood, fire or famine to meet a deadline in the publishing process of your novel. People will be depending on you.

dedication [See also Acknowledgements/Back matter/Front matter]

A dedication, dedicating your novel to some person(s)—even your cat—can appear on the preliminary pages, or in some cases, on the back pages after the text of your novel. Think carefully about dedicating your novel to your current live-in lover. It could be dodgy if you move on. BIANCA

Keep your dedication short and sweet.

defamation

Defamation is exposing someone to hatred, ridicule, contempt or injuring his or her reputation through writing. If you're with a traditional publisher the copy editor will look out for this. If you are self-publishing be very careful you do not defame any person(s) through your writing. DIGBY

description [See also Characters/Imagery/Setting]

Description is using words—creating visual pictures—so your readers can visualise what you are writing about. There are three main kinds of description: character, landscape and object. Use concrete nouns, strong verbs and carefully chosen adjectives. DAPHNE

Don't just write a heap of descriptive text when you can't think of anything else to write. Description should be vivid and have a purpose.

desktop publishing [See also Self-publishing]

Desktop publishing, also called desktop production, is a term when computer software packages are used to produce fully made-up copy. JOSH

Knowing how to desktop publish is useful for marketing if you are self-publishing.

detail [See also Characters/Setting]

Detail is important in many different ways when you're a writer. For example: writing detail into descriptions, the detailed reading needed in the nitty-gritty, line-by-line reading of your contract, and noting detail in the copy editing stage of your novel. GINA

Similes and metaphors are great tools to use when you're capturing detailed description for your novel.

detective novels [See Crime fiction/Whodunits]

deus ex machina [See also Plot]

Deus ex machina means *god from the machine*. *Deus ex machina* refers to the ancient Greek theatre when actors playing gods would be lowered by machinery onto the stage to provide a resolution for the plot. If your characters need a helping hand from a god, fate or coincidence to complete their quest you need to acknowledge your plot is not working and do some revision. For example: If your detective meets a psychic who tells her the name of the killer on the last page. Or, Great Aunt Edith leaves your protagonist a fortune in her will when your protagonist is down to her last dollar. PANDORA

development editor [See also Editor]

A development editor is a term frequently related to a non-fiction and fiction editors. A development editor is commonly called a literary consultant in the fiction world. Sometimes they are known as a commissioning editor or a substantive editor. Their job is to develop a manuscript at the level of content i.e. plot, narrative, characterisation, scenes, setting and writing style. They will read a manuscript and prepare an assessment report at the content level, making suggestions with the aim of helping the author reach the potential of their novel. BILL

dialect [See also Dialogue]

Dialect is the sound of speech, and vocabulary used by people in a certain area or country. Writing dialect is not easy. Try saying it aloud as you write. *Less is more* is a good rule to follow when you are trying to catch dialect on the page. BILL

dialogue [See also Attributions/Speech tag/Quotation marks]

Dialogue is words spoken in conversation. Dialogue can show character, give information, add colour and move the story forward. Writing good dialogue can bring your novel to life. Create variety and pace by using actions to indicate to the reader which character is speaking. Avoid using a grab-bag of verbs associated with speech or conversation. However *asked* is good to use for a character asking questions, *shouted* is good to use for when a character is shouting and *said* is a great standby. Along with the modern trend for writing novels, many writers have decided to bypass speech tags entirely. BILL.

Dialogue that does nothing but convey information should be suspect.

diary [See also Blog/Journal/Notebook]

A diary is usually a dated, daily written record of activities, but it can be used to record personal thoughts. It's written from the point-of-view of the writer. A diary format can be used as a structural device for a novel. DAPHNE

Personal diaries are useful to trace ideas and emotions of past events and times to use in your writing.

dictionary [See also Thesaurus/Tools of the trade]

A dictionary is a vital tool for a writer. Never put your faith in a spell check. Keep a dictionary close at hand to look up the spelling and meaning of words. VIOLET

digital backup options

[See also Cloud/External storage device/USB]

Digital backup options are options to use if you're writing your novel using a computer or electronic device. These options include a system backup, a file backup and online storage. There are multiple choices if you decide on a file backup using external storage devices and/or online storage. The choice you make will depend on your budget, the quantity of writing you're producing and your attitude to security for your writing. JOSH

digital detox

A digital detox is advisable for writers if you want to write that novel. Try avoiding social media or at least cut the time you spend on it. Limit the time you spend sending and receiving emails, tweeting, posting or using other social media. JOSH

There are apps that will prevent you using social media while you should be writing 'the' novel. Give them a trial.

digital publishing [See also e-book/e-publishing path]

Digital publishing is publication of a work (your novel) for an electronic or digital environment, usually in e-book format. JOSH

digital rights [See also e-book/e-publishing path]

Digital rights are the rights to reproduce the work (your novel) in a digital/electronic form. For example: an e-book. JOSH

dinkus [See also Transitions]

A dinkus is a typographical symbol used on a page to denote transitions between scenes. Using dinkuses breaks chapters for ease of reading. BILL

direct speech [See also Quotation marks/Speech Tag]

Direct speech is words spoken by someone. The author writes the words as if a character actually said them. Quotation marks are used for the actual words spoken in direct speech. When you begin direct speech with quotation marks, you must also close with quotation marks. Words not actually spoken are placed outside the quotation marks. The first word in direct speech begins with a capital letter and punctuation. DIGBY

discoverability [See e-publishing path/Panel copy/Self-publishing]

Discoverability is the new buzz word used in online marketing. You need savvy marketing so your e-book can be discovered in the sea of novels in cyberspace. PANDORA

DIY cloud [See also Backup/Cloud]

DIY Cloud is a term referred to when you save your novel file. Email it to yourself and hey presto, a virtual version is stored on your computer and ready to retrieve if you need it. Blogs can also make useful places to store drafts of your novel. Create a draft post and paste your manuscript into it. DAPHNE

DIY publishing [See also e-publishing path/Panel copy/Self-publishing]

DIY publishing or hybrid publishing are terms used by authors when they control the publishing of their novels through independent, mainstream publishers and self-publishing. To DIY publish you need to be energetic, have plenty of time and cash resources as well as project management skills. When you take a DIY approach to publishing you need a professional approach to your work. Your novel will need professional editing, a must-buy cover design, panel copy and a layout to compete with other novels on the market. Marketing and distribution channels are vital to ensure the successful sale of your novel. LEE

Self-publishing is relatively easy. The marketing and distribution to earn the cash you out-lay is the difficult part.

dog [See also Characters]

A dog in a novel can be an agent for change, a metaphor for unconditional love. A dog can also be a wise confidant who sets the hero or heroine on the right path in life. A dog written in a novel can assist the hero or heroine to learn to trust again, build relationships and human contacts. GINA

Cats when written into the plot of a novel can also be change agents.

Don't talk about your novel! [See also Shop-bought-cake lies]

Don't talk about your novel—except to other writers—until it's completed or published, is sound writerly advice. If you talk about your novel before it's completed you'll think you've written it. It's perfectly possible to talk your novel into a quick death. GINA

DPI

DPI is a design abbreviation for *Dots Per Inch.* This is a measurement of image resolution. (Low-resolution images may be suitable for web use, but generally appear grainy or blurry in print.) LEE

This is useful information for online marketing of your novel.

draft [See also 3-drafts process]

A draft is a completed version of a novel. First drafts are often called rough drafts. JOSH

Be prepared to write and rewrite numerous drafts before you're ready to submit or self-publish your novel.

drop

Drop is a publishing term to mean the distance from the top of the page to the type area. LEE

Dropbox

Dropbox is a cloud storage provider. When you have installed *Dropbox* on your computer it appears as a folder on your screen. You simply drag or copy your files into the folder. Anything in the folder is backed up on Cloud and can also be accessed through your laptop or devices. To share your drafts or documents right click on the folder in your Dropbox, select *Dropbox*, then *Share This Folder* and follow the prompts to enter the email addresses of the people you want to share with. GINA

Using the Dropbox feature is a useful way to share your writing for comment and editing with writerly friends.

drop down [See also Transitions]

Drop down is a printing term for double-spacing between scenes (leaving an extra blank line on the page). It's used as a visual cue to show you've completed one plot action and wish to move your characters to a different location or time. You can reorient your reader after the *drop down* with the next sentence.

For example: The next day... or After breakfast... BILL

drop initial

Drop initial is a publishing term for an initial capital extending over several lines. Drop initials are usually design features at the beginning of chapters. JOSH

dump bins

Dump bins are temporary marketing containers used in real-time bookshops. PANDORA

dust jacket [See also Cover design/Self-publishing]

A dust jacket is the paper cover wrapped around a hardback novel. In the past a dust jacket was the first encounter a would-be buyer would have of a novel. Dust jackets contain four pieces of information: the title of the novel, the name of the novelist, the imprint of the publisher's identity, and the merchandising and ISBN information hidden to the human eye in the bar code. Very few novels are published today with dust jackets. DIGBY

A hard cover copy of a novel wrapped in a beautifully designed dust jacket is something to be treasured.

dystopian [See also Speculative Fiction]

Dystopian is a word to describe bleak fantasy, horror or sci-fi genres where everything is disastrous. Dystopian fiction is a popular genre. JOSH

Utopian is the opposite of dystopian.

E

e-book [See also e-reader/Digital publishing]

An e-book is a digital form of a book that can be read on an e-reader—an electronic device. Book buyers and readers can buy e-books, or borrow and download them from libraries. JOSH

e-book design [See e-publishing path/Self-publishing]

e-book design is flexible and can be manipulated in many ways. It has a one-page design to fit and be displayed on the screens of e-readers and devices. A single page of text fits the screen perfectly. Most e-readers were designed to mimic the size and proportion of a paperback page in order for e-books to be familiar to readers. Readers can choose or change the size of their font, increase line spacing, margins and more. Because of the flowing nature of the text of an e-book, each screen or *page* will never have a set page number. The numbers will not match up with a print book nor will they be the same from one device to another. They may even change on a single device if the reader adjusts the settings. Creating and making changes to an e-book file can take significantly more time than typesetting and making changes to a print book. This is due to the fact that an e-book formatter works with the raw text and the source code of the file. JOSH

e-book file changes can take longer than a print book and usually require additional costs.

e-publishing [See also e-publishing path/DIY publishing/Self-publishing]

e-publishing, aka digital publishing, is the new rapidly expanding digital landscape where publishers, co-publishers, subsidiary publishers and individual authors publish their novels to promote, sell and deliver the electronic version. When a traditional publisher accepts your novel, there will be clauses to cover electronic publication. JOSH

e-publishing path
[See also e-book/DIY publishing/e-publishing path]

The e-publishing path involves you, the author, having control over the content, cover, layout, panel copy, pricing and marketing of your novel. You can either undertake the complete e-publishing path yourself, or outsource providers and services to do part or the complete publishing process. However, you can decide on the panel copy—title, cover, spine and back cover copy—chapter lengths, numbers and headings. And you choose the pricing. Within certain limits you decide how much to charge for your novel. You'll need to check similar novels and decide whether to match, undercut or ignore their pricing. You can market your novel or employ a service to do the marketing and publicity. JOSH

Mainstream publishers have snapped up many self-published e-authors.

e-reader [See also e-book/e-publishing path]

An e-reader is an electronic device used to read an e-book. There are many different brands to choose from and some will only take specific e-books. LEE

editing [See also Copy editing/Editor/Self-editing]

Editing is the process of revising your manuscript to correct errors and achieve the best possible novel. It means altering the order of words, sentences, paragraphs and whole sections of text. One school of thought is to edit your manuscript later—even the next day. Get that first draft down. Another school of thought is to edit-as-you-go. Your choice! Consider employing a professional editor if a publisher or agent likes your first submission and you're short on time. GINA

If you've some cash to invest you'll feel confident when a professional editor has edited your novel.

edition [See also Hardback/Paperback]

Edition is the publishing term for a new publication of your novel, a changed and reset reprint. It can also be a publication of your novel produced in a different format such as hardback, a different paperback size or an e-book. BILL

editor [See also Editing/Rewrite/Self-editing]

An editor is a self-employed person, or employed by book publishers to acquire and edit manuscripts for production as books. An editor will evaluate the flow, logic and the overall message to help an author shape their novel and breathe life into it. An editor is an author's collaborator. They care about your novel and your best interests. When an editor flags a problem in a novel they are usually right. Remember you don't have to accept their suggestions to fix the problem as long as you fix it. Traditional publishing houses employ professional editors with varying skill levels and titles e.g. production, commissioning, structural, development and copy editors. Proofreaders edit after the typesetting process. In a traditional publishing house your editor is your representative when they work with senior editors, the production manager and the sales and marketing team. VIOLET

Editors are humans with whims and moods. What they reject one day they may accept the next. Members recommend you employ a qualified editor to make your novel the best it can be if you are self-publishing.

editorial style sheet [See Style sheet]

e.g. [See also i.e.]

e.g. is an abbreviation of the Latin words *exempli gratia*, for the sake of an example. In English it means 'for example'. It is followed by an example of the preceding word or phrase. It is sometimes written without full stops (eg). DIGBY

Do not confuse e.g. with i.e.

electronic rights [See also Contract/Digital rights]

Electronic rights, also called digital rights, is a term used in a contract or agreement with a publisher to determine the electronic publishing of your novel. The term 'electronic rights' is constantly changing with new IT developments. For example: it may include access to publishing on Facebook, YouTube, Twitter, websites, blogs, and Smart Reads. BILL

elegy

An elegy is a mournful or melancholic poem often written about the dead. DIGBY

elevator pitch [See also Logline/Pitch/Premise]

An elevator pitch is five or six lines that expand the logline to summarise your novel—think a 3-minute time-limit pitch at the most. It's a pitch you can use when you meet an agent or a publisher in an elevator, or an editor at a party and they ask, *So what's your novel about?* Make sure you capture the genre and the conflict and a bit about the main character(s). PANDORA

Try describing your book in less than one minute—even 30 seconds. Cut fluffy adjectives, explanation of your novel's structure or how you came up with the idea.

ellipsis (. . .) [See also Punctuation]

Ellipsis (...) is a punctuation mark—three spaced dots—to let a reader know you've left some words out of a quote. If it is used in text it denotes an omission—it can indicate that a sentence has trailed off... You will find ellipses used frequently on back cover blurbs. JOSH

em [See also En/Dash/Hyphen]

An em is a printing and publishing term used for the space occupied by the letter *m* in any particular typeface and point size. It's called em because *m* is the widest letter of the alphabet. The em-dash is used as a separator, amplification, and to signify abrupt change. Beware of an epidemic of em dashes. DIGBY

email [See also Cover letter/Query]

Email is an electronic method of communication. Treat emails like official communication. Use capital letters, punctuation, correct grammar and writing conventions—contractions can be acceptable. Check you have the correct email address. Use a specific subject heading that makes sense. Be concise, but give enough information so the recipient knows what you mean. People who read a lot of emails don't have time to work out what you mean. Read the email before you send it. Is it saying what you want to say? Be polite when you sign off. cc (carbon copy) the email to yourself so you have a record of your communication on hand. PANDORA

Remember the delete button is always close. Work out what you want to say. If you don't know, don't send an email.

emoticon

An emoticon is punctuation put together to represent a basic graphic such as a smiling face. Emoticons are used to express emotions such as happiness or sadness in text messages in social media. For example: :-) ☺ or x-(☹ BIANCA

It's best to avoid using emoticons in professional communication.

en [See also Em/Dash/Hyphen]

An en is a printing term for the space occupied by the letter *n* in any particular typeface and point size. It is half the width of an em. The en-dash (or en rule) is a linking device. DIGBY

end matter [See Back matter]

endnotes [See Back matter/Footnotes]

end papers [See also Dust jacket]

End papers is a publishing term for a pair of leaves (pages) at the beginning and end of a book. On a hard-back book a leaf of each pair is pasted to the inside and back covers to provide extra support for the binding. In some high-end priced hard-backed editions of novels, the end papers are included in the design of the book. VIOLET

epigram

An epigram is a terse, witty saying or a poem. For example: Rope is thick but string is quicker. Spike Milligan. DIGBY

epilogue

An epilogue is the summary or conclusion of a book. It often brings the different parts of a novel together. Most modern novels don't have an epilogue. DIGBY

epigraph [See also Prelims]

An epigraph is a quotation that appears in the preliminary pages or at the beginning of a chapter or scene of a book. DIGBY

epistolary fiction [See also Diary/Journal]

Epistolary fiction is telling a story through fictional documents such as letters, diaries, journals et cetera. Your novel may consist entirely of such documents, or may be semi-epistolary—mixing documents with first or third-person narrative. Today there are many document formats—emails, social media messages and blog posts—writers can choose to tell their stories. The word epistolary derives from the Greek word epistle, meaning a letter. DIGBY

Readers trust documents and they give an authenticity to your novel.

epitaph [See also Historical novel/Prelims]

An epitaph is a quotation or message written on a tombstone to commemorate a person's death. Most epitaphs give information—names, dates, and names of parents or children. For example: Here lies Violet Harris. Published author who never missed a deadline. VIOLET

Tombstones in cemeteries are excellent research material—you can collect names, dates and information when you're writing an historical novel.

eponyms

Eponyms are names that come from people's names. For example, the word biro used for a ballpoint pen, was named after Laszio Biro, the inventor of the ballpoint pen. Eponyms can also be the brand name for an item, which is used as a common name for the product, or its use. For example: when the product name *Kleenex* is used for a tissue of any type and when the product name *Xerox* is used as a verb meaning to make copies. BIANCA

It's usually okay to use brand names in popular novels but you might like to check this out with the specific companies owning the brands.

erotica & erotic fiction [See also Pen name]

Erotica and erotic fiction are different categories and genres. If you're writing erotica or erotic fiction check with publishers' websites for writers' guidelines, requirements and restrictions. Read erotica and erotic fiction to understand the difference and to gain an idea of how explicit it is. Erotic fiction is romance—fully fleshed-out stories that contain a love/relationship arc. Writing erotic fiction is like any other genre fiction so approach it with a professional attitude. Generally erotica fiction is all about lust with an occasional love story. The story arc can be a quick sexual encounter with some inner reflection, a larger life lesson, a month of self-expression for characters, et cetera. VIOLET

If you're writing about BDSM (bondage & discipline, sadism & masochism) practices, research is crucial.

et al.

et al. is from the Latin *et alibi* meaning *and elsewhere.* It has a second meaning from the Latin *et alii* meaning *and others.* It is sometimes written without the full stop. DIGBY

et cetera (etc.)

et cetera comes from two Latin words, *et cetera* meaning *and so on.* Etc. is an abbreviation for the words *et cetera. Etc* is sometimes written without a full stop. VIOLET

Members voted (8-9) to use the two-word combo et cetera rather than the abbreviated version etc in this publication.

euphemism

A euphemism is indirect words and expressions used for things that are embarrassing or unpleasant to say. For example: *dropped off the perch* meaning a person has died. VIOLET.

eulogy

A eulogy is a speech given at a funeral honouring the person who has died. They are not easy to write. VIOLET

exclamation mark (!) [See also Punctuation]

The exclamation mark (!) is a punctuation mark used by writers to add dramatic effect to their writing. It was once called the *note of admiration* meaning *mark of wonder*. Exclamation marks were known as screamers in the newspaper trade. It was considered bad form to end a sentence with one. The old school of writing favoured restraint and suggested exclamation marks should hardly ever be used. *Less, as ever, is more.* However, in the Internet age of social communication exclamation marks are making a comeback. *Thanks!!!!* is considered friendlier than *Thanks.* **DIGBY**

exclusive rights [See also Contract]

Exclusive rights are secondary rights in a publishing contract. If you sign exclusive rights to territories you agree on, your publisher will be the only one who can exploit these rights. When a publisher negotiates these rights to publish your novel in another country these rights can be a valuable source of revenue for writers. PANDORA

exposition [See also Plot/Show don't tell]

Exposition is the term used for detail and information written in a novel. Beware of too much exposition. Don't write chunks of exposition! It can slow the plot and make for tedious reading. Use action to give information to the reader rather than write long passages of exposition. BIANCA

Take note of the adage 'Show don't tell.'

external storage device
[See also Backup/Cloud/Digital backup options]

An external storage device is excellent for storing electronic files. Thankfully prices are going down even though storage capacity is going up. The device simply plugs into your computer and can back-up your entire computer every day. The latest models of external hard drives are neat looking devices, easy to pick up and take with you in an emergency. Check the size you'll require. JOSH

Several members have external hard drives and consider them the ideal backup solution combined with their faithful USBs.

eyestrain [See also eXercise]

Eyestrain is a hazard when you're writing a novel—especially if you're using a computer. You can develop eyestrain from focusing on your computer screen for long periods. Use the 20/20/20 rule. For every 20 minutes you're working at your computer, look away at an object 20 feet away for 20 seconds. To prevent glare, use soft lighting—lampshades and natural light filtering through curtains or windows. Your computer monitor should be in a position so glare from your light source doesn't bounce off the screen. Take a nap or go for a walk to rest your eyes. Uncorrected vision impairments can also lead to sore and irritated eyes. Have regular eye checks. DAPHNE

F

fable [See also Anthropomorphism]

A fable is a traditional short story that has a moral at the end. In a fable animals and insects act like humans with human thoughts, feelings and actions. *Aesop's Fables* are popular fables. George Orwell's satirical novel *Animal Farm* (1945) is a fable in which cunning and treacherous pigs rule over the more honest and gullible farm animals. GINA

F2F [See also Branding/Marketing]

F2F is an abbreviation for a face-to-face meeting. A F2F meeting is extremely useful for writers when they communicate with editors, publishers and colleagues. A F2F meeting should be valued highly. It's vital in connecting with people in your novelist role. Think about the image you want to project to sell your novel. For example: a live-in-an-attic-suffering novelist, a hot-and-out-there novelist, or a confident literary I-know-what-I've-written novelist. Beg, borrow, or steal gear and accessories to connect with your image. For example: wear casual-stylish black, up-market gear, or high-end jewellery. Designer dark glasses are must-have gear for a hot-and-out-there novelist look. DAPHNE

You never get a second chance to make a first impression.

Facebook [See also Social media]

Facebook is one of the most *social* of social media sites. Facebook has hundreds of millions of active users. As well as interacting with your readers you can set up a page that is open to the public to publicise your books. Facebook is a good place to mention promotions you might be doing, such as making your book free for a while on Amazon. It can also be useful for driving traffic to your website or blog. LEE

> *Think carefully when you use Facebook. You can never retrieve what you've posted.*

fact [See also Factoid/Historical fiction/Research]

A fact is the most current piece of proven information accepted by a society. DAPHNE

factoid [See also Fact/Historical fiction/Research]

A factoid is a small or little known fact. Factoids can give a novel a quality of authenticity. Researching background material and discovering little-known facts can shape the structure of a novel. DAPHNE

factual accuracy [See also Afterword/Foreword]

Factual accuracy is not absolutely essential for writers of historical novels. It is the story—the gaps in the facts—that will keep your readers turning the pages. If you tell a convincing story readers will be prepared to forgive you even if they know the facts are dodgy. Remember history is a writer's playground where you can have fun and unleash your imagination. Dates can be rearranged and altered as well as locations where characters appear and/or meet. You can have inventions occurring years before they actually were invented. You can change the date of battles if you're in a boring stretch of your novel. Several minor historical characters can be combined into one to simplify the narrative, or a minor historical character can take centre stage. Fictional characters can be at the heart of real historical events. Background inaccuracies will usually be forgiven by your readers, however watch your inaccuracies don't impact on the plot. Include a foreword or afterword explaining where you have taken liberties with the facts. Undermine expected criticism from history buffs by acknowledging that like your readers you're also human. DAPHNE

Do the mea culpa thing. State that any errors are entirely your fault.

fair use [See also Contract]

Fair use is a term for provision of the copyright law allowing brief passages from a novel to be quoted without infringing on the owner's rights. LEE

fairy tales

Fairy tales about soft-hearted wood-cutters, evil step-mothers, wolves, dwarves, sleeping or hardworking princesses, kind frogs and beasts that turn into handsome princes and rescue captive princesses can be reworked. They offer numerous starting points and ideas for novels of many different genres. BIANCA

fan fic

Fan fic, or fanfic, is a modern term that refers to works (novels) that borrow characters, worlds, or both from an existing creative source: a book, a television show, comic, a Grimm's or Hans Christian Anderson fairy tale et cetera to create an unauthorised derivation. Writers have been doing this for the millennial. For example: Virgil's *The Aeneid* is a story based on a minor character from the writing of Homer. JOSH

Many beginning and well-known authors have, and are writing fan fic works.

fantasy fiction [See also Science fiction/Speculative fiction]

Fantasy fiction in its traditional structure has been top of the bestseller charts for a long time. The setting is a key element in traditional fantasy fiction, such as Epic, Heroic and other subgenres. The setting is the other world a writer creates with its geography, landscape, politics, law, culture and society. These other worlds resemble historical—particularly the medieval—period. A complex setting is vital. The fictional world you create plays a major role in what you write. It will dictate the characters you create, the action that drives your plot and a world your readers can visualise. Traditional fantasy fiction has archetypal characters such as elves, dwarves, dragons, orcs, goblins, trolls, ogres and giants. When you write fantasy fiction you've complete freedom to invent magical characters, places, objects and language. In Heroic fantasy (also called sword and sorcery) there is a hero/heroine, setting out on a quest for a talisman. Along their journey the hero/heroine has many adventures in a fight for good against evil. JOSH

Sorting and inventing names for characters can be the first step in creating your new world.

fantasy subgenres [See also Speculative fiction]

Fantasy subgenres have emerged in the last decade and have become bestsellers in novels as well as films, TV and digital games. Fantasy subgenres cover a broad spectrum under the umbrella of Speculative fiction and are constantly evolving. Urban fantasy, also known as contemporary, modern or real world fantasy, has magical beings and supernatural forces unbalancing a world we are familiar with. Harry Potter is an example of urban fantasy. Other subgenres of fantasy fiction are Horror or Dark fantasy, New Weird, Comedy fantasy, Magic Realism or Magical Elements, Steampunk and Arthurian fantasy. Arthurian fantasy encompasses stories about King Arthur and Knights of the Round Table characters—Merlin, Guinevere, Lancelot and Morgan Le Fey. JOSH

fantasy trilogy

A fantasy trilogy (three linking books) occurs when authors develop their first novel into a trilogy. Throughout the trilogy the world and main characters set up in Book One have to be consistent and fit within an overarching story within the trilogy. *For example: the Harry Potter series. Each book contains its own storylines and plot points involving the conflict between Harry Potter and Voldemort until their final confrontation.* JOSH

With a little bit of luck you may find your trilogy morphs into a best-selling series.

fax plot device [See also Plot]

A fax plot device can be included in your novel if you're writing a novel set in the time when faxes were important forms of communication. For example: a plot point could be when a vital fax arrives and the protagonist doesn't receive it. Or the antagonist sees the fax and destroys it. BIANCA

feedback [See also Criticism/Partial/Writers' groups]

Feedback—a friendlier word than criticism—usually happens in writers' workshops. Writers offer suggestions to other writers on how to improve their writing. You can give feedback to fellow writers on novel outlines or drafts—partial or completed. Be specific in your suggestions and give examples. Giving constructive, concise feedback helps you to look closely at your own writing. Receiving constructive feedback is valuable for writers. It gives you an idea of how your audience follows and visualises your writing. However, don't feel you have to fix your writing every time you receive feedback. VIOLET

Think carefully before you offer to edit a writers' group member's novel and give the writer feedback. It's very time consuming and you may end up minus a writerly friend.

fewer/less

Fewer and Less are words that can be confusing for writers. They both mean smaller but in slightly different ways.

* **Fewer** is applied to a number and should be used when describing things you can count. For example: There were fewer members at the Shelly Beach Writers' Group than expected.
* **Less** is applied to quantity. Less means not as much, a smaller quantity. Less should be used when describing things you can't count. For example: Building high-rise on the Shelly Beach foreshore means less land for public recreation. DIGBY

Use fewer with plural nouns (fewer members) less with singular nouns (less land).

fiction [See also Commercial fiction /Literary novels]

Fiction is a literary work created by a writer's imagination. It's writing based on something that is not true or real—it is make-believe. Fiction is divided into two categories—literary and commercial (or contemporary) fiction. The line between these two categories is blurred. Many commercial or contemporary novels are written as literary fiction. BILL

figure of speech [See also Hyperbole/Metaphor/Simile]

A figure of speech is an expression with an unusual or original meaning. Figures of speech add oomph to your writing. Figures of speech include metaphors, similes, and hyperbole. JOSH

file backup [See also Cloud/External storage devices/USB]

A file backup involves copying your files using external storage devices so they can be accessed on another computer or replaced on the original computer after a failure or breakdown. External storage devices include CDs and DVDs, USB flash drives and external hard drives. CDs and DVDs are excellent for saving and sharing files with writerly colleagues but not so brilliant for storage. On the upside they're small, inexpensive and portable. On the downside they're fragile, can be damaged easily and are limited in capacity. JOSH

film rights [See also Contract/Logline]

Film rights are options a film company will offer for a novel so they can make the film adaption. Some of the options never turn into film deals but you will probably get to keep the money, and you might be able to sell the options again. If a mainstream publisher publishes your novel, the publisher, or your agent will negotiate film rights. If you're self-publishing the negotiating is up to you. BIANCA

Always have the logline for your novel on hand so you can sell the film rights to your novel.

the final chapter [See also Chapter/Chapter outline/The Pay-off]

The final chapter is a blissful stage to reach when you're writing a novel. There are thousands of writers who start novels—only a few manage to finish. Most novels need to have the conflict and issues solved by the final chapter. If you're writing crime fiction you need to solve the crime. In the final chapter of a romantic novel your engaging hero and heroine should be in places they want and deserve to be. However, some writers of contemporary and literary novels write final chapters where the reader is left wondering about the ending and this is perfectly acceptable. LEE

finding the right publisher

[See also Genre/Literary Agent/Submitting your novel]

Finding the right publisher is not easy. It's important to understand where your novel fits in the market. Read novels in the same genre, or novels similar to yours. Take note of the publisher. Check out publishers' websites and catalogues. Attend writers' conferences and festivals to meet agents and editors and hear what they are looking for. PANDORA

Some publishers won't accept your pitch unless you have an agent. In today's market members suggest you give yourself a time-line in which to find the right agent or publisher. Then think about self-publishing.

finite verbs [See also Infinite verb/Split infinitive/Verb]

Finite verbs have a subject. For example: Dogs dig in the sand. Writers write anywhere. Editors edit manuscripts. DIGBY

the first line [See also Opening paragraph]

The first line of your novel is possibly the most important sentence you will ever write. It must work like a baited-hook to reel your reader into your novel. Some editors have been known to only read the first sentence of a submitted novel. If it interests them, then they read the next, hopefully the next and the next, and then the first paragraph. Possibly the first page. Hopefully the editor will then request to see your novel and when it is published the reader will buy or borrow the novel. Don't spend too much time searching for the first line for your novel. You might never get past the first line. Start your novel. A first line will come to you later during the writing of your novel. However, if you write the *perfect* first line, it could be quoted for centuries such as:

* All happy families are alike. All unhappy families are unhappy in their own way.' (Tolstoy, *War and Peace.*)
* It is a truth universally acknowledged, that a single man in possession of a good fortune must be in want of a wife. (Jane Austen, *Pride and Prejudice.*)
* Call me Ishmael. (Herman Melville, *Moby-Dick.*)
* Last night I dreamed I went to Manderley. (Daphne Du Maurier, *Rebecca.*)

* Mr and Mrs Dursely of number four Privet Drive, were proud to say they were perfectly normal, thank you very much. (J.K. Rowling, *Harry Potter and the Philosopher's Stone.*)
* The book was thick and black and covered with dust. (A.S. Byatt, *Possession.*) GINA

flash fiction [See also Writing classes and workshops]

Flash fiction is a writerly term to describe a story that sits below 1000 words in length. Different publishers and anthology requirements have different ideas of what is flash fiction. Writing a piece of flash fiction is an excellent writing task or exercise to hone your craft. JOSH

It's always best to check guidelines before you write flash fiction for a specific publication.

flashback [See also Flash–forward/Transitions]

Flashback is a writing technique that uses information from your characters' pasts. It's often useful and sometimes necessary in the structure of your novel. A writer can use flashback to alternate between the present and the past to tell what happened before the story started, and/or why your protagonist or characters had a particular issue. It should literally be a flash-back-in-time to get information across to your reader so you can proceed with the flow of your story. The word flashback was used in about 1918 to describe the recapitulation of an earlier scene in a film. It was soon used to describe a revival of the memory of past events in a novel. Instead of writing pages of flashback, try to thread important information through the main plot as your write. Recall backstory from a character's angle when he or she is thinking back, or use dialogue. Always make sure it is absolutely clear to the reader when the flashback starts and finishes. The useful word now can help the reader come out of the flashback. Obvious chapter headings and scene breaks also make it easier for the reader to recognise flashbacks in time in your story arc. Signpost the fact you're revisiting the past with a relevant link. For example: The dog thought back to when... GINA

Take care you don't overdo flashbacks. They can slow the action and confuse your reader.

flash-forward [See also Flashback/Transitions]

Flash-forward is a writing technique that uses information about your characters' future. Use signposts to indicate you're visiting the future so you don't confuse readers. For example: It was the year 2020. JOSH

flawed characters

[See also Character-driven novel/Character profiles/Characters]

Flawed characters make great main characters. They're more interesting to create and develop. Flaws in a character give plenty of material to write about. GINA

It's a good idea to love your characters, flaws and all. You have to live with them a long time.

folios [See also Self-publishing]

Folios is a design term to be aware of when self-publishing. It refers to running heads and/or footers on interior book pages that orient the reader by displaying the page numbers (centred or along the page edge), the title of the book (usually on the left page) and optionally, the chapter title or author name (on the right page). VIOLET

font [See also Formatting]

Font is a word that refers to a complete set of typeface and point size. There are an incredible number of unusual and beautifully designed fonts. Take care when selecting fonts for your cover if you're self-publishing. Many fonts have copyrights. JOSH

Some writers become obsessed with fonts. Don't waste valuable time in discovering and playing with fonts.

footnotes [See also Back matter/Endnotes]

Footnotes give a reference to the source of an author's research. They are supplementary information placed at the bottom of a page. Reference footnotes are indicated with a symbol such as an asterisk for the first footnote, a dagger for the second, et cetera to link to the specific text of the book. Footnotes rarely appear at the bottom of commercial novels. They're usually found at the end of a novel. However, if you're writing a scholarly literary novel, conscientious publishers and editors may require you to use footnotes at the bottom of pages. DIGBY

There is a computer feature to add footnotes.

foreign rights [See also Contract]

The foreign rights of your novel are usually sold to international publishing houses to enable them to translate the work (your novel) into their native language, or to publish their own edition in agreed territories if the language remains the same. Foreign rights can provide a valuable revenue stream. If your novel is published by a traditional or Indie publisher check your contract and know your entitlements. PANDORA

foreshadowing [See also Crime fiction/Chekov's rifle]

Foreshadowing is a writing technique. It gives clues to outcomes in your novel. You can foreshadow surprises that will spring out in your writing later. Keep your foreshadowing subtle. For example: foreshadow an unusual crime weapon (not an obvious bloodied knife on the kitchen table) in the early chapters of a crime fiction novel to keep your readers guessing who has used it and why. VIOLET

foreword [See also Afterword/Self-publishing]

The foreword is text written at the front of a book. Foreword comes from two words, fore (front) and word. It was first used in English in 1842. A foreword is not used in the majority of commercial novels. DIGBY

You can use a foreword in the back of your self-published novel but it will become an Afterword.

formal language [See also Informal language]

Formal language is used when people are using their best language. For example: in the pulpit, in an academic lecture and in the company boardroom. Formal language is charac-terised by long complete sentences and Latin and Greek vocabulary. DIGBY

format [See also Self-publishing]

Format is a publishing term that refers to the shape, size and general appearance of a book. For example: paperback, hardback, e-book. DIGBY

formatting [See also Proposal/Pitch /Submitting your novel]

Formatting is a process to transform your writing into a readable product. It's important to present your writing correctly for reading by your writing group, when entering competitions, and when submitting your novel. Follow agents' and publishers' formatting guidelines but the following is a general rule. Use double line spacing and an easy font to read. Times New Roman size 12/14 pt. is an industry standard. Left-hand and right-hand margins should be approximately 2.5 cm. You should have a title page with your name and address, phone number and email address, the title of your novel and the approximate number of words. The title and page number should appear on each page of your manuscript. It's usual to put them in the header or footer—and use automatic page numbering. Each chapter should begin on a new page. Dialogue and new paragraphs are indented. Do not have a double space between paragraphs. Only use a double return for scene breaks if the break is unclear. Text following a gap (including dialogue) is not indented. If you want to italicise a word italicise it. Do not underline. Underlining was used in the past because there was no way of italicizing a word on a typewriter. There is only ONE space, not two between sentences—two spaces was industry standard before word processing became the norm. LEE

Request submission guidelines from specific agents and publishers. And don't use two spaces between sentences. Editors, agents, publishing houses and especially formatters loathe this practise.

fortuitous fiction [See also Marketing]

Fortuitous fiction is a marketing term for a novel that hits the market at the perfect moment in time. For example: a prime minister's daughter writes a novel about a prime minister being deposed by his female deputy and the novel is released when a prime minister is actually toppled by his female deputy. PANDORA

FPO [See also Cover design]

FPO is a design abbreviation meaning *For Position Only*. FPO is used when an image is a place holder, i.e. an image that is not print quality has been uploaded. LEE

four-colour printing [See also Self-publishing]

Four-colour printing is a publishing term for printing using the three pigmented primary colours and black: cyan, magenta, yellow and black. LEE

fragments [See also Sentences]

Fragments, also called sentence fragments, are sentences without subjects or verbs. They can give rhythm to your writing. BIANCA

free writing [See also Writer's block]

Free writing, also called stream-of-consciousness writing, is a useful technique for a writer. It's the act of writing nonstop for a pre-planned length of time. It's writing to get thoughts down. Time yourself to distract your internal editor. Don't cross out. Don't edit. Just write. Scenes for your novel can often begin in free writing. BILL

Free writing is a useful activity if you think you're coming down with an attack of writer's block.

freelance writing [See also Recycled bin writing]

Freelance writing is when a writer submits articles and short stories to publishers and publications. The term *freelancing* dates from the twelfth century when a knight, (who lost his alliance with a landed lord) would offer himself as a mercenary—a lance for hire. As you write your novel contemplate using research, discarded pieces of writing or rejected chapters to rewrite as articles or short stories to promote your novel. Give your characters new conflicts and obstacles. Research markets where you can place this writing. PANDORA

Freelance writing can bring in income and/or create publicity for your novel.

frisson [See also Romantic fiction/URST]

Frisson is a word used by writers of romantic novels. Frisson refers to sexual tension (the heart of a romantic novel) between the hero and heroine. Frisson comes from a French word meaning a short, sudden feeling of fear, surprise or excitement. It's very important to keep your frisson frissoning when you're writing romantic novels. BIANCA

front matter [See also Acknowledgements/Author bio/Dedication]

Front matter, aka prelims, refers to the content that comes in the front of a novel. Front matter can include the copyright, title, subtitle and imprint pages, as well as the dedication, acknowledgements, an author biography, table of contents and maybe a foreword. The publisher will decide the front matter, if a mainstream or independent publisher publishes your novel. If you're self-publishing you can decide the content to go on the front pages. VIOLET

full submission [See also Partial/Query/Submitting your novel]

A full submission is a term for submitting a complete manuscript to an agent or editor as opposed to a sample or a proposal. BILL

Never send an agent or a publisher a full submission unless it's requested.

full point [See also Full stop]

Full point is a publishing term for a full stop. DIGBY

full stop (.) [See also Punctuation]

Full stop (.), also called a period, is a punctuation mark. (Period is Greek for road going around). A full stop is used to mark the end of sentences that aren't questions or exclamations. It was originally used to mean take a long pause. Editors will use a publisher's house style for the correct use of full stops when writing titles, headings, headlines, et cetera. DIGBY

the funny hat [See also Characters]

The funny hat is a phrase used by writers to describe the particular piece of characterisation they use to make a character instantly memorable for their reader. It could be a character's speech or clothing et cetera. For example: Dickens (in *David Copperfield*) uses Mrs Micawber's dialogue to make her memorable. She is constantly reminding us that she'll never leave Mr Micawber. DIGBY

G

galley [See also Proof]

A galley, or galley proof, is a publishing term for early typeset copy. A galley was named after the long metal trays originally used for holding and storing the lines of metal type for printing. Today the term galley is used for a proof of any size and is vanishing in the digital publishing age. VIOLET

genre
[See also Crime fiction/Cross genre/Historical fiction /Romantic fiction]

Genre—category—fiction is commercial fiction that fits into specific categories. It's the literary form a novel falls under and is placed for marketing, sales, shelving in libraries, bookshops and on screens. Classify your novel under a genre when you're pitching your completed novel to an agent, publisher or are intending to self-publish. There are many novel genres e.g. crime, sci-fi, fantasy, speculative fiction, paranormal, romance, westerns, erotica, erotic, YA (young adult), historical fiction and horror to name a few. New genres and subgenres are being created constantly. If you've written a cross genre you name the primary genre, then add one, two or more genres. For example: use one adjective *historical* as the primary genre, and add the second genre *thriller*—historical thriller.

Masses of readers love reading novels that fall into their favourite genre divisions, rating them as quality reads. GINA

If you're writing a genre novel with the hope of winning the Man Booker or Pulitzer Prize don't hold your breath.

gerund [See also Verb]

A gerund is a grammatical word for a verb when it is used as a noun by adding *ing* to the stem. *For example: Violet's editing is spot on.* VIOLET

ghostwriter [See also Freelance writer]

A ghostwriter is an author who writes a book that is credited to another person. Ghostwriters are usually employed through agents or publishers. Ghostwriting is not like writing a biography (digging up information) but it's an excellent way to earn money by plying your craft. As a ghostwriter you need to be a diplomatic and sensitive listener to bring out the best of your client's story and transfer it to the printed page or onscreen. VIOLET

Be prepared to put your ego aside and not worry about fame if you become a ghostwriter.

GMC

GMC is a writerly abbreviation for goal, motivation, and conflict. You need to know your character's GMC in order to write a page-turner. BIANCA

goals [See also Deadline]

Goals are important when you're writing a novel. A writing goal can get you to the last page. Set yourself writing goals.

Aim for a word count goal of 500 to 1000 words, a set number of hours, or a specific number of pages and scenes to complete each writing session. GINA

the Golden Age [See also Cosy crime fiction/Whodunits]

The Golden Age refers to detective fiction novels—strong on plot and puzzle that were written in the 1920s and 1930s. The Golden Age detective novels were written by women who proved themselves experts as they wrote about the gentle art of violent death. The central characters were amateur sleuths that happened onto crime-after-crime in their own small corner of the world. Dorothy L Sayers created her amateur sleuth, Lord Peter Wimsey; Agatha Christie—Hercule Poirot and Miss Marple; Margaret Allingham her snobbish detective—Albert Campion. The amateur sleuths were sent to investigate, deduct and inevitably solve the crimes. The Golden Age of detective fiction formed a reading habit in the public and established the convention of detective fiction or whodunits. The two-dimensional aspect of detective fiction offered relaxation, diversion and reassurance for readers—comfort reads. VIOLET

good/well

Good is an adjective. It modifies a noun. Well is an adverb, it modifies a verb, adjective or another adverb. For example: When a *good* chef cooks *well*, a perfect pie is the result. DIGBY

grammar [See also Parts of speech/Punctuation]

Grammar is a set of rules. The rules are used to make words, phrases, clauses and sentences function well. Sentence structure, parts of speech, as well as punctuation come under the heading of grammar. There are two main schools of grammar—modern and traditional. Understanding the rules of grammar makes it easier to talk with editors and writerly colleagues about your writing. The modern trend is to ignore some traditional rules of grammar. Don't panic about grammar. Buy reputable how-to books on grammar and study them. BIANCA

You have to know a rule before you can break it.

grammar check [See also Grammar/Spell check]

A grammar check is a feature in computer software packages. According to the computer-designed grammar check, green squiggly lines can appear under your sentences on the computer screen to indicate you've used incorrect grammar. You can heed or disregard this computer feature. BIANCA

Remember this feature is not designed for creative out-there writers of novels.

graphic novel [See also Storyboard]

A graphic novel is a novel where the story is told through drawings, graphics, design and text. Plot, character and setting—elements of a print novel—are vital in a graphic novel but are told through drawings as well as text like in a comic book. LEE

grasshopper writer

A Grasshopper writer is a writerly term for a writer who works on other writing projects as well as writing their novel. For example: you could be writing a how-to article, posts for a blog, or working on a non-fiction book as well as a romantic short story. It's a good idea to use the *Urgency versus Importance* grid attributed to Stephen Covey and Dwight W Eisenhower to list projects.

Use headings:
* *Not urgent but important*—(schedule time to do it)
* *Urgent and important*—(do it now!)
* *Not urgent or important*—(don't do it.)
* *Urgent but not important*—(delegate or refuse to do it.) GINA

Be flexible! Pencil entries in your diary then you can erase them.

the Greengrocer's apostrophe [See also Apostrophe]

The Greengrocer's apostrophe refers to a depressing misuse of the apostrophe. People such as greengrocers are often confused in the use of the apostrophe when they write daily signs e.g. *Apple's $4 a kilo.* DIGBY

guidelines [See also Formatting/Online slush pile/Submitting your novel]

Guidelines are contributor or manuscript instructions for writers. They show a writer how to plan a written or online submission to an agent, publisher, publication, competition et cetera. They include required themes to write to, format, layout and the required word count. Guidelines to submit a novel can be found on publishers' websites. BILL

Follow guidelines carefully.

gutter [See also Self-publishing]

Gutter is a publishing term for the centre of a spread (space) where two pages meet. This should generally be at last 0.75 inch (2 cm). It will be more for books of 300+ pages so the words aren't swallowed into the crease when the pages are bound. LEE

H

had [See also Flashback/Plu-perfect tense]

Had is the past perfect of the verb *have*. It's a significant word to use when you go into flashback. Use *had* at the start of a flashback to show you're going back in time. For example: In the year 2012 Jane had six lovers. As soon as possible drop *had* and write as if the scene is in the present. Using *Now...* will make it crystal clear when you come out of flashback. Resume direct dialogue so it makes it an immediate story again. **BIANCA**

Using too many hads *can deaden a scene.*

handle [See also Character-driven novels/Characters/Flawed characters]

Handle is a word used by writers to describe the narrator's view in their novel. For example: Sylvia's *handle* on the affair is that... Writers also use the word handle as a metaphor when writing their novel. For example: I can't get a handle on my plot. **BIANCA**

handwriting [See also Diary/Journal/Notebook]

Handwriting is an ancient form of communication. Handwriting says something about the writer whether the writing is fine copperplate, pencil-written sentences with mistakes neatly crossed out, or a list of hastily scrawled words in biro. In the past we were judged by our handwriting with all its elegant swirls and squiggles, eccentricities and idiosyncrasies such as making perfect little circles or heart shapes above the letter *i*. Writing by hand was a regular way of communicating through letters, postcards, diaries and notes. Handwriting had add-on value. When love letters were written it was not the handwriting that counted but the heart and soul of the writer that came with the letter. The days of ink-stained fingers and hand cramp, scrawling away on a nine-hundred-page-or-more novel (e.g. Victor Hugo's *Les Miserables*) has vanished in the distant past. VIOLET

Resurrect the joy of using a beautiful pen dipped in ink, skimming over the surface of blank pages catching ideas, phrases, words and sentences a la Jane Austen in the 1800s.

hard copy [See also Formatting/Full submission/Submitting your novel]

Hard copy is the printed manuscript of your novel. It's copy produced in typed form or a computer printout. BILL

When you've completed your novel keep a hard copy of your manuscript ready to give to an agent or publisher if they ask for it.

hardback [See also Dust jacket /Paperback]

Hardback is the term for the superior format of a novel at a high-end price. It's a book to be valued if you enjoy the smell and feel of a book. A hardback novel can have a dust jacket packed with artwork, publicity and information. It will have quality paper design and layout. Hardbacks are a durable physical format of a book (in contrast to the consumable paperback and the intangible e-book) and make excellent gifts. They are aesthetically pleasing, and can give the buyer or receiver the thrill of acquisition and ownership. Signed early edition hardback copies are to be treasured. DIGBY

hash tag (#)

The hash tag began as a symbol for the weight *pounds*. Today it is used to mark key words, a label or comment on the social media platform Twitter. LEE

HEA

HEA is a common writerly acronym for *Happy Ever After*, an ending of a romantic novel that (hopefully) leaves readers happy and satisfied. BIANCA

head–hopping [See also POV/Time–slip novel]

Head-hopping refers to writing from the viewpoint of two or more characters in the one paragraph. Head-hopping can be very confusing for readers. Writing different chapters or sections in your novel from different POVs (Points-of-view) is a different matter. GINA

helper [See also Antagonist/Characters/Protagonist]

Helper is a writerly term for one of three main character roles in your novel. The *helper* character(s) act as a catalyst, a force for change. For example: The dog in the novel *The Shelly Beach Writers' Group* is Gina's critical friend and confidante in her search for a new life. BIANCA

hen lit [See also Chick lit]

Hen lit is a term to describe novels written about women

who are over thirty. Hen lit novels are not to be confused with Chick lit. Hen lit, contemporary novels are entertaining reads but deal with serious issues and messages underlying the plots. DAPHNE

HFN [See also Romantic fiction]

HFN is a writerly acronym for a *happy-for-now* ending used in romantic novels that end realistically. BIANCA

hero's journey [See also Plot]

The Hero's Journey is a model or structure for a plot based on the mythic story arc. It's a model of rising action in three parts.

1. The first part, the *ordinary world* is when the hero is called to adventure, refuses the call, and when the mentor is introduced.

2. The second part is the *crisis* when the hero encounters the first threshold with tests; meets allies and enemies and the hero encounters the *inmost cave*—an ordeal.

3. The third part is the climax—the resurrection. The hero is on the road back and he returns to the ordinary world. JOSH

Read books by Joseph Campbell and Christopher Vogel for more information about the Hero's Journey.

high concept [See also Premise]

High concept is a literary term referring to high-concept fiction that has a knockout hook. The belief is that a high-concept novel sells easily since its premise can be described in a single phrase or sentence. For example: Snakes loose on a 627. Usually high-concept novels elicit a strong reaction when pitched. PANDORA

historical fiction [See also Factual accuracy/Fact/Factoid/Research]

Historical fiction is a genre based around history. It has all the elements of a commercial novel (theme, plot, characters) but is set in an imagined or real historical setting. Research adds authenticity to your novel but the story is the most important element. Research can reveal not only the details of the period but will help you get a feel of the unique flavour of the time. For example: the Regency period 1811-1820 if you're writing a Regency romance. The trick is to include historical details and use the flavour of the language and idiom of the time. Some authors write successful historical novels that only contain cherry-picked details from history. They find the small kernel that makes the remaining description feel real. They weave threads of factual information into their novel so they can build convincing characters and plot. Use short descriptions rather than pages of researched detail. Take care with character names, titles, costumes, language, conventions and constrictions of the period. And don't forget to research the social structure of the time such as the hierarchy of servants. **DAPHNE**

Use a dictionary of historical slang to check out the language of the time.

hobby [See also Self-publishing/Submitting your novel]

A hobby such as *writing* the *novel* is cool and most times a comforting pastime. Many writers spend their weekends, spare time—even years—writing *the* novel. You can write a novel anywhere—in bed, in the bath, outdoors and at any time. *Writing* the *novel* is an economical hobby. You only need a pen and notebook—or a computer, printer, reams of paper, ink jet cartridges and postage. Postage costs are necessary when your novel is completed and you submit it to a mainstream or independent publisher. Obviously you don't need postage costs if you submit your finished novel to publishers online. However, with the changing publishing industry you can take the route of DIY publishing. Your novel can be uploaded in a microsecond and launched into cyberspace. Once a publisher accepts your novel or you are selling it online, your hobby is transformed into a profession. BILL

Many writers have a novel inside them. Extracting it can be a painful process that can last for years.

homonyms [See also Dictionary/Homophones]

Homonyms are words that are spelt the same but have different meanings. For example: bow. DIGBY

homophones [See also Dictionary/Homonyms]

Homophones are words that have the same sound, but different spellings and meanings. The word homophone comes from two Greek words—*homos* meaning same and *phonos* meaning sound. For example: knight and night, right and write, paw, pore, poor and pour. DIGBY

Use a dictionary or a style guide to solve any spelling issues. Do not rely on a computer spelling checker.

hook [See also The first line/Opening paragraph/Query]

A hook is a metaphor used frequently by writers—especially writers of fiction. You need a hook to sell yourself and your novel when you write queries and submissions. A baited hook is also necessary to grab your reader in the first line, the first paragraph and the first page of your novel so they will keep reading until they reach the last page. DAPHNE

Remember you're selling your novel to people whose first inclination is to say no!

horror fiction [See also Crime fiction/Speculative fiction/Suspense]

Horror (dark) fiction is a popular fiction genre. It can be about vampires, supernatural ghosts, villains, demons, monsters, and zombies et cetera. This genre demands great skill on the part of the writer so your reader suspends disbelief. Your challenge as a writer of horror fiction is to horrify your readers—but make your plot believable. Atmosphere is a prime ingredient. Try to build atmosphere and end with a fantastic scare. LEE

Don't forget—for every death there must be a consequence.

How do I know when my novel is done?
[See also How long is a novel?/Word count]

How do I know when my novel is done? is a question frequently asked by writers. The answers to four questions can help a writer reach a decision.

1. Are you exhausted? (Written enough and ready to move forward?)
2. Have you followed your plot timeline to the end?
3. Have all the threads of your plot come together?
4. Is there something you still want to say that comes within the parameters of your novel?

If you've answered *yes* to the questions 1, 2, and 3 but *no* to question 4 you are not *done* with your novel! VIOLET

A work of art is never finished—just abandoned. Move on.

How long is a novel? [See also Chapters/Novella/Word count]

How *long is a novel?* is a common writerly question similar to the question, *How long is a piece of string?* A novel can be anything from 50,000 to over 700,000+ words. Your novel should be just as long as it takes to tell the story. From our survey (rough-average-per-page word count) and interviewing people from the book industry, publishers are unlikely to look at anything shorter than 80,000 words. However, they may prefer a novel closer to 100,000 words i.e. readers expect a biggish book for their money. Sometimes readers expect certain lengths for certain genres. Readers could be looking for a minimum of 100,000 words for a fantasy genre. Check out the length of novels selling well that are similar to yours. Many e-books are 50,000 or less. BILL

Just keep writing until your story is down. Don't worry about counting words or length of chapters as you write. Edit, fine tune, chop and change later.

house style [See also Indie publisher/Mainstream publishing]

House style is a guide that covers preferred spelling, punctuation, usage and layout. Individual publishers have their own house style. If you have a deal with a mainstream or small publisher your novel will be edited according to the publishers' guidelines. DIGBY

If you are self-publishing it pays to keep a style guide for your novel and be consistent.

hybrid author
[See also Indie publisher/Mainstream publisher/Self-publishing]

A Hybrid author is a writerly term for an author who has their novels published using a traditional or mainstream publisher, a small publisher and/or self-publish.

hyperbole [See also Figure of speech]

Hyperbole comes from an ancient Greek prefix *hyper* used to mean *over, above, excess. Bole* was a Greek word meaning *a ball. Hyperbole* was the Greek word for the arc a ball follows when it's thrown high into the air. Hyperbole was added to the English meaning *deliberate exaggeration*—over-the-top (OTT). A writer can use hyperbole to create humour or emphasis in their writing. For example: Extracting his novel was an agonising process. DIGBY

hyphen (-) [See also Em/En/Hyphen strings]

A hyphen is a small en (-) dash that joins words together. It can make one word of two. It can glue prefixes like *non* to whole words to make a complex word. For example: non-fiction. Hyphens are also for words that modify nouns. For example: self-published novel, back-seat driver. Usage varies from dictionary to dictionary. A word can change over time from two words, tea bag (1898), to one word with a hyphen, *tea-bag* (1936), to a word with no hyphen *teabag* (1977). S*ource: Oxford English Dictionary*. The en—can also stand in for *till*, or to express a span of time, place or number. For example: 9.00-12.00, Shelly Beach—Kingston, 1959-2009. DIGBY

Computers have a feature you can adjust for the use of hyphens.

hyphen strings [See also Hyphen/Hyphenation]

Hyphen strings are used in contemporary writing to link words in a sentence. For example: It was a will-this-fit-into-my-novel thought? PANDORA

hyphenation [See also Hyphen/Hyphen strings]

Hyphenation is a word to represent dividing words with hyphens. The British style of hyphenation tends to divide words into meaningful parts. The American style tends to divide words into syllables. DIGBY

When you're placing your hyphens watch out for eccentric placement e.g. mans-laughter.

I

I/me [See also Grammar/Pronouns]

I and Me can be confusing pronouns for writers when they want to use them in a sentence. For example: a writer can waste time wondering whether I or Me is the correct usage in a sentence such as *Digby and* me *went to the meeting.* If you split the sentence in two, you'll find out whether *I* or *me* is being used correctly. VIOLET

For example:

Digby went to the meeting. ☑ *Me went to the meeting.* ☒

I went to the meeting. ☑ *Digby and I went to the meeting.* ☑

idea [See also Brainstorming/Mind mapping/Notebook]

An idea is necessary to begin a novel. Enjoy the hunt to find a kernel of an idea that kick-starts your novel. A good time to start a novel is when an idea has been fermenting in your mind for a long time. Writers usually get ideas very easily; they collect them like magpies. The secret is to trap them and keep them safe for an idea-drought time. Keep a file or list of ideas on your computer or in your notebook. Take care when you share ideas. There is no copyright on ideas but it's annoying to find you have a good idea for a novel and another writer has beaten you to it. However, many successful novels have been written based around the same idea that was used to start another novel. **DAPHNE**

Keep a notebook, pen, and flashlight on your bedside table to jot down ideas you get between 3 and 6am.

i.e.

i.e. is an abbreviation of the Latin words *id est* which means *that is*. It is sometimes written with one full stop (ie.) or two (i.e.). The modern trend is to disregard full stops. **DIGBY**

imagery [See also Description]

Imagery is cool description you paint with words on a page to create an image in your reader's head. Some writers play the scenes of their novels in their heads like a movie. Then they transcribe these scenes on to the pages of their novels so it enters their reader's mind. The reader then adds their details to the imagery. **BIANCA**

imagination

Imagination is a creative mental ability writers of fiction possess. Imagination enables a writer to live in another world while they're writing their novel. A writer's imagination creates believable settings, characters and plots to translate into words on paper or on the screen. When readers read these words they are (hopefully) transported into another world. A writer needs to constantly use their imagination while they revisit and revise their novel. **DAPHNE**

Imagination is an unappreciated gift to a writer.

imprint [See also Front matter]

The imprint is a publishing term for the name and address of a publisher or printer, or both. The imprint is usually included on the preliminary pages of a novel. LEE

income [See also The business of writing/Grasshopper writer]

Income refers to the amount of money earned by an author. It rarely adds up to a living wage and offers no financial security. Most writers disregard this fact; work at paying day jobs and beg, borrow or steal time to write. Some writers commit to full-time writing. They write a wide-range of content, or work at writerly careers connected to their writing e.g. lecturing, tutoring, editing et cetera. In spite of poor financial returns, writers value their writing and only feel secure when they have a work-in-progress. BILL

inconsistencies [See also Crime fiction/Editing]

Inconsistencies will create holes in your plot and weaken it. They can jolt your reader out of your story. For example: if you're writing crime fiction and one detective is mentioned briefly in the beginning of the story but only comes into the story again on the last four pages of your novel. Copy editors are very good at picking up inconsistencies in your novel such as your protagonist's eyes changing colour, and a character not being where he should be i.e. he's in Perth instead of being in the Shelly Beach café. GINA

You have to accept when you're writing your novel that you know what your characters are doing—when and where they are doing it—but your readers may not because you've neglected to fill in the details.

indie author [See also Hybrid author/Self-publishing]

An Indie (independent) author is a trendy term for an author who is self-publishing as well as having their novels published by mainstream and independent publishers. Once upon a time a self-published author was considered an egotist who ended up with a garage full of unsold novels or a self-indulgent memoir. Not so today. Indie authors know the Indie movement in publishing is here to stay. JOSH

The most successful self-published authors are those who plan their project carefully and set themselves realistic goals.

indie publishers [See also DIY publishing/Hybrid author]

Indie, also known as independent publishers, are small exciting and adventurous publishers looking for authors. The advances may not be large (frequently non-existent), however if the sales go well there is a chance for an author to earn royalties—maybe make the bestsellers list. BILL

An Indie publisher may be lean but it doesn't mean they're not professional. An author needs to submit their best possible manuscript.

infinite verb [See also Finite verb/Split infinitive/ Verb]

Infinite verb is the grammatical term for a verb that usually begins with *to*, and is not the main verb in a sentence. For example: The dog dug a hole to bury his bone. The writer edited her novel to meet the deadline. DIGBY

informal language [See also Contractions/Dialogue/Formal language]

Informal language is language used between families, friends, colleagues and characters in your novel. It is characterised by shortened and colloquial words. For example: Chill out, Cool, Awesome. BIANCA

intensifiers [See also Modifiers]

Intensifiers are words or phrases that emphasise or boost the effect of other words. *Very* is a very commonly used intensifier. *Absolutely, definitely, positively* are other examples of intensifiers that are used to emphasise words. DIGBY

Try to make minimum use of intensifiers.

interior monologue

Interior monologue is writing about a character's inner thoughts and feelings. When you use interior monologue to show a character's mental processes you can add psychological impact to a novel. Many novels are written using a narrator's internal dialogue as their structure. These novels ask a lot of readers. It is also industry standard that internal monologue/dialogue is italicised to differentiate between the spoken word. GINA

Be wary of using too much interior monologue. It can make for a dull read.

interior monologue scenes [See also Interior monologue/Scene]

Interior monologue scenes are when characters or the narrator take time out from the action to process or summarise events, or simply to reflect on life. BILL

Interior monologue scenes give readers a chance to catch up with what's happening.

interjection [See also Punctuation]

An interjection is a word or a phrase that expresses a strong feeling. For example: Wow! If you're writing a commercial novel you could be using a heap of interjections. BIANCA

internet right [See also Electronic rights/Digital rights]

Internet right is the right to post an author's work on a website or on another electronic platform i.e. to distribute or allow the distribution of excerpts of a novel via the Internet. LEE

interviews [See also Branding/Marketing/Talks]

Interviews have a nightmare rating for authors whose strength is in expressing themselves through the written word. Be prepared. Don't wing it. Contact the producer, journalist or reporter of your radio, TV or press interview. Have a chat. Get an idea of the questions he/she wants to ask. Prepare information to promote your novel. Tape yourself! If your interview is live in a radio studio or office allow plenty of time to reach the destination. Take your novel, notes and a bottle of water with you. Fight the nerves. Be natural. Be prepared to provide off-the-cuff personal information. Have fun or be serious—whichever mood matches your novel—to promote it. TV interviews can be especially traumatic. Pass TV spots if you don't feel the publicity is worth the trauma. However, if you decide to accept the opportunity of a TV interview, obtain information from the producer before your interview. Find out if the segment will be taped or live. Ask for the list of questions to be asked. Before your interview, think of three main points about your novel. Work these points into concise sound bites. PANDORA

Practice your interview presentation with a friend or in front of a mirror.

intruder [See also Flawed characters/Character profiles/Characters]

Intruder is a writerly word for an *alien,* or *stranger* character who penetrates the closed circle of characters in your novel to create drama. For example: A toxic friend confessing her affair with her best friend's husband. Three things can happen to the intruder: they are repelled at the threshold, evicted following their penetration of the closed circle, or assimilated into the interior of your novel. BILL

inverted commas [See Dialogue/Quotation marks]

IPR [See also Contract/Publishing Rights]

IPR is an abbreviation for Intellectual Property Rights. IPRs are rights associated with anything you create (your intellectual property), which you can exploit to gain revenue. If you've a contract with a publisher, the publisher or your agent will be negotiating these rights on your behalf. If you're self-publishing it will be up to you to do the negotiating. LEE

IRC [See also Cover letter/Submitting your novel/Query]

An IRC is an abbreviation for International Reply Coupon. An IRC should be included with any correspondence or submission to a foreign publishing firm. These coupons can be purchased from post offices. An IRC allows the editor to return your novel or reply to your query letter by mail without incurring a cost. BILL

irony [See also Style]

Irony is the mildly sarcastic use of words to mean the opposite of what is expected, or to underline the truth. Irony is often funny. There are many ways you can use irony in a novel.

For example: you can give a character ironic dialogue such as *Perfect weather* when it's raining cats and dogs. You can also write a complete ironic novel. DIGBY

ISBN [See also Self-publishing]

An ISBN—an abbreviation for International Standard Book Number—is the thirteen (or for older titles, ten) digit numbers found on the copyright page of a book. It's unique to that title in that format, in a specific language and country, or countries. A hardback will have a different ISBN to the paperback and e-book edition of the novel. The US hardback will have a different ISBN to the Australian hardback if a different publisher publishes the book, even though they are the same title. ISBNs make for efficient communication between publishers and booksellers. Each number contains ten digits divided into four groups separated by spaces or hyphens.

* Group 1: National language or geographic area.
* Group 2: The publisher's prefix.
* Group 3: The title number that identifies the book itself, its edition and binding.
* Group 4: The *check* digit to pick up errors in the other 9 digits.

If you're self-publishing and want to sell your novel you need to buy an ISBN number for each of your published books. LEE

Use the ISBN number to identify your novel when you're ordering copies from your publisher for your friends and family.

italic

Italic is sloping type used for emphasis. DIGBY

it's/its

It's and its are two three-letter words that frequently become grammatical errors. It's (with the hanging apostrophe), is the abbreviation for *it is*. For example: It's time to finish your novel. Its is the possessive. For example: The dog cut its paw. VIOLET

Use the apostrophe = i rule. When you write or see the apostrophe in the word it's, *insert the letter i before* s. *Check if the sentence still makes sense.*

J

jargon [See also Dialect/Language]

Jargon is language used by a particular group of people who live, work, study together, or have a particular mutual interest. If you're setting your novel in the world of fashion, banking, or bird watching et cetera it will pay to research (books, Internet, TV and films) the jargon used to add authenticity to your novel. For example: A dress with a knicker-flicker skirt. (Fashionista jargon.) BIANCA

journal [See also Blog/Diary/Interior monologue]

A journal contains reflective writing and is not wholly determined by daily events. It can be a private record or written for others to read. A utilitarian journal can be sufficient for your needs as a writer. It can collect ideas, valuable notes, inspired fragments, leads or outlines of what you may use when you write later.

Your journal can also work as an interior monologue to reflect on events and people in your life's journey. You can use your journal to make lists, jot down ideas and thoughts, explore feelings, and keep records of dreams and travel. Your journal can also work as a scrapbook; a collection of print memorabilia that decorates your life's journey.

A journal can also be a collection of handy hints, tips, recipes, and information that captures your life and times. Excellent fodder for your novel writing. **DAPHNE**

Search for old journals in second-hand shops. They can be valuable resources and give you ideas to structure a novel.

justified type [See also Unjustified type]

Justified type is a printing term for type set flush against both right-hand and left-hand margins producing vertical alignment at both right and left margins. **VIOLET**

There is a computer feature to justify type.

K

kerning [See also Font]

Kerning is a designer term that means to manoeuvre type. It is an adjustment of space between pairs of letters to achieve tightness or evenness of appearance, particularly when capital letters are used in headings. Type may be kerned or unkerned. High-end desk-publishing software packages have features so operators can work with kerning. JOSH

Writers who purchase desktop software packages can become obsessed with fonts and design type.

kill your darling [See also Editing/Self-editing]

Kill your darling is a phrase attributed to William Faulkner and used in editing. The word murder is frequently substituted for kill. A Stephen King quote: *Kill your darlings, kill your darlings, even when it breaks your egocentric little scribbler's heart, kill your darlings.* The quote means to be prepared to reconsider some of your writing—writing you think is unbelievably brilliant—and edit it for the good of your novel. Many writers cut thousands of words, pages and pages of their much-loved-novel-to-be in order to improve their novel. BILL

You won't find out what to cut until you've written it. Keep your cuts and put them in a file. They could be a start of another novel.

knew/new [See also Homonym/Tenses/Verb]

Knew and *New* are frequently confusing words for writers.

* **Knew** is the past tense of the verb *to know*. For example: I knew the Writers' Group meeting was going to be a disaster.
* **New** is an adjective. For example: He knew she was looking for a new husband. GINA

If you use these words incorrectly, a spell check won't pick them up.

L

language [See also Sentences/Style/Word]

Language is made up of words and sentences. Words and sentences are amazing inventions for writers. Writers use words and sentences to write. The language you use in your novel is connected to your writing style. For example: nouns, verbs, adjectives, adverbs, hyperbole, metaphors, and similes et cetera. BIANCA

The longer a writer practices their writing the better they will be at wielding words for their readers.

laptop [See also Computer]

A laptop is a light, portable and compact computer. Laptops are useful if you write your novel while travelling on public transport or you like to write outdoors, in libraries, cafes, et cetera. Before buying a laptop, visit a computer store and trial various models. Compare the feel of keyboards, screen displays and price. VIOLET

Do not use a laptop in the bath!

lay/lie [See also Homonym/Tense/Verb]

Lay and *Lie* are words that can be totally confusing for a writer. Remember these words have different meanings, and both *lay* and *lie* have more than one meaning.

* **Lay** means to put or place except when you write about birds laying eggs. For example: Adrian's chickens didn't *lay* many eggs this week. *Lay* is a transitive verb and it must have an object (bed) to complete its meaning. For example: I *lay* down on the bed.

* **Lie** as an intransitive verb meaning to rest or recline. It does not need an object. For example: The dog will *lie* down. *Lie* can also be used as a noun meaning an untruth. For example: The *lie* Kenneth told was practically believable.

* **Lay** and **Lie** become totally confusing verbs when they're used as verbs in different tenses. For example:
  To lay: to put or place; Lay – Laid – Had Laid
  To lie: to rest or recline; Lie – Lay – Had Lain GINA

Look for a grammar book with table headings: Present tense, Past tense, Present participle and Past participle to understand the correct use of these two confusing verbs with their very different meanings.

layout [See also e-book/Proof/Self-publishing]

Layout is a term in printing and publishing for the arrangement of type and/or headings and illustrations on a page. Graphic designers are responsible for devising the layout of a novel. Book-template software packages can produce excellent layouts if a competent operator uses them. Content, size, the two-page design of a printed book, and its readership should be considered in order to produce a good layout. Each set of facing pages is known as a spread. This is how a reader will see the pages spread out.

For a conventional novel a grid, or template, is printed to make sure all dimensions are accurate and consistent. An e-book has a completely different layout to the printed book. JOSH

Make sure your layout is easy to read when you check page proofs of your novel.

lead time [See also Deadline/Mainstream publishing]

Lead time is the time between the planning of a book and its publication date. VIOLET

The lead time can take about nine-eighteen months if you have a book deal with a mainstream publisher, or a shake of a lamb's tail if you're self-publishing.

leading [See also Kerning]

Leading, pronounced led-ding, is a design term for the blank horizontal space between lines of text. The term is used when the design of a book is being discussed. In the days when printers prepared type with letters on blocks of moulten metal, they could add extra space between lines by inserting strips of lead. VIOLET

legacy publisher [See Mainstream publisher]

legacy publishing [See Mainstream publishing]

legend [See also Myth]

A legend is a traditional story handed down from the past. It's focused around a famous person, place or event. It could be true or invented. Heroes such as Ned Kelly (Australia), Robin Hood (England), and Johnny Appleseed (USA) are legendry characters in stories. Many novels use fictional legends—celebrities, criminals and sporting stars—as their protagonists. LEE

legs [See also Marketing]

Legs is literary lingo—a marketing word used in publishing. A publishing team will be asking if your novel has legs? Will your novel walk out of a bookshop, off a shelf or from a screen? PANDORA

If you're told your novel hasn't got legs, the agent or editor believes it won't stand out among competition.

licensing [See also Contract]

Licensing is granting permission to a publisher to publish your novel in the formats and territories agreed during you or your agent's negotiations. If you are undertaking DIY publishing you will do your own negotiating to license your novel. LEE

life of your novel [See also Phoenix novel]

The life of your novel, once it is published, can be short or long—and it can be resurrected. Some readers will love your novel and find it inspiring. Other readers will dislike it. And then again some readers will neither like, nor dislike it.

You can't please everyone. Get started on your next novel.

lightning/lightening

Lightning and Lightening are confusing words. Lightning is the sudden electrostatic discharge during an electrical storm. Lightening is to illuminate or brighten, or to make a colour a lighter shade. JOSH

line editing [See also Proofreading]

Line editing, also called proofreading, is editing your writing line-by-line for spelling, grammar and punctuation. It's a painful process. However, it is absolutely essential to do after you've completed the final draft of your novel. VIOLET

Holding a ruler under each line as you read will pick up errors—especially if you work from the bottom of the page up.

listening [See also Café writing/Observing]

Listening is a vital skill for a writer. Be invisible. Leave your ego behind and deep-listen as a compassionate human being. This will result in collections of anecdotes and stories to retell and use in your writing. DAPHNE

lists [See also Bullet points/Grasshopper writer]

Lists are useful for writers. To-do lists are great for focusing on writing tasks at hand. For example: A structuring-and-completing-a-novel list, a three-goals-for-today list, and what-I like-about-my-antagonist list. Lists can be used as literary devices. They can become structural engines to drive a novel. Lists can also be a mixture of a writer's shower-thoughts and must-do life stuff. A publisher's program of books published in the past is called *the backlist*. Publishers also refer to their new allocation of published books as *the* list. Cross-off lists (prioritising life stuff) started about the 1920s as jazzy new ways of getting more done. If you get stuck writing your novel, write a non-fiction book that gets on the *Top 50 non-fiction book list*. For example: *101 Dog-care Tips*. Make tick-off-as-you-go, bullet-point lists or ignore lists altogether. Instead go-with-the-flow and trust everything will get done in time. If you're into concrete lists in order to get time to write, follow the 120-second rule. If a task can be done in 120 seconds don't list it! Do it! GINA

Beware of becoming an obsessive list-maker i.e. one who makes lists from lists. Just write!

literary agent [See also Agented material/Editor/Genre]

A literary agent is a person contracted by an author to find a publisher for their novel and conduct the business side of publication for them. A literary agent is paid by the author after sales of the manuscript. It's great when you get an agent who believes in your novel. Many agents will work with you to suggest changes to your novel before they submit it. Some agents will only handle writers who write certain genres. Once an agent sells your novel to an editor, the next editor to edit the book is unlikely to love your novel as much. This is where an agent is useful in resolving issues and smoothing bumps on the author's, and the novel's behalf. BILL

Agents have become endangered species over the past few years due to the changing publishing industry. Some agents have diversified and assist authors in DIY publishing.

literary device [See also Flashback/Foreshadowing/Transitions]

A literary device is a term used to describe techniques a writer uses—the writer's tools they keep in their bag of tricks when they're writing their novel. For example: flashbacks, foreshadowing, metaphors and simile et cetera. DIGBY

literary novels [See also Fiction/Commercial fiction]

Literary novels are considered to be more serious (slower paced and more carefully crafted) than contemporary or commercial novels. A literary novelist is considered to have paid more attention to style. They can explore important themes, current issues, and develop settings and characters more deeply than contemporary or commercial novelists.

Literary novels usually have a hard cover or they are a trade paperback—an oversized paperback with a designer cover. Writers who write what is categorised as a literary novel can enter their novels for major literary prizes. DAPHNE

Group members believe literary novels can be challenging and entertaining. Contemporary or commercial novels can also be challenging and entertaining reads. It all depends on the mood you're in when you read them.

logline [See also Elevator pitch/Film rights/Marketing]

A logline is a one-sentence selling line that summaries your novel. Write a logline to excite and/or intrigue potential buyers of your novel. It should reveal the genre and conflict of your novel in fewer than ten words. BILL

long fiction [See also Novella]

Long fiction refers to a novel of accepted word length in contrast to a novella, or a short story—short fiction. Some extra-lengthy works of long fiction are over 700+ pages—brick-like books. They can make extremely comforting long reads. DIGBY

lose/loose

Lose and Loose are confusing words. Lose is only used as a verb—it means to suffer a loss, to be deprived of, to part with or to fail to keep possession of. Loose is used mainly as an adjective, and describes things that do not fit tightly. (e.g. The screw is *loose* fitting.) When loose is used as a verb, it means to release (e.g. Let *loose* the dogs.) VIOLET

lower case lettering [See also Upper case lettering]

Lower case lettering is a term used in word processing and typesetting software for small letters. In the early days of printing, printers prepared type by placing letters one by one. Sets of alphabetical ordered letters were kept in large wooden cases placed on sloping racks. The smaller letters the printer used more often were kept in the lower section of the case. They became known as lower case letters. VIOLET

M

mainstream novel [See Commercial fiction]

mainstream publisher

[See The Big Five publishers/The Big Six publishers]

mainstream publishing

[See also The Big Five publishers/The Big Six publishers]

Mainstream, often called traditional, or legacy publishing involves a dedicated professional team offering you support through the nine months or longer to publish your novel. Editors, cover and book designers, copy editors, proofreaders, marketing experts, sales teams, and publicists work together to help you produce the perfect novel, get it into bookshops and online so it sells well. In mainstream publishing, the publisher will involve you in the editing process and proofreading. They select the cover design (they may ask your opinion), the layout of the book, whether to issue it in hardback, paperback and/or e-book and to which market it will be exposed. They decide on the promotional work undertaken to wholesalers, retailers and readers—where it hits the tables and shelves of an ever-diminishing list of bookshops and/or online bookshops. The marketing team will organise media interviews and promotions. They will send out copies of your novel in the hope it will receive favourable reviews to help it on its way. Being picked up by a major publisher is a huge boost for a novelist. There are still amazing possibilities with mainstream publishers for new writers and ideas. BILL

Don't assume your first submission through the mainstream route will succeed and be prepared for a glacial-slow publishing process..

margins

Margins are the white space around the edges of the pages—top, bottom and sides—generally one inch (three cm). The bottom margin is usually slightly larger than the top. VIOLET

marginalia

Marginalia is notes scribbled in the margins of books or in the margins of your work-in-progress. For example: cross references, additional thoughts. DIGBY

mark-ups [See also Editing symbols]

Mark-ups are the marks used to show the three key concepts of editing—insertion, deletion and substitution. Use a caret to show an insertion. Use a forward slash to delete one character and a horizontal straight line to delete more than one line. To show a substitution is needed, delete the character(s) using a forward slash or horizontal line, then write the correction after the deletion in the margin. VIOLET

Learn editors' mark-up symbols and use them when you're editing your own and colleagues' writing. This method of editing is still viable and useful in the technological age.

marketing [See also Discoverability/Marketing timelines/Marketing tools]

Marketing is getting your book noticed in order to sell it. Getting your novel published is the first step, but marketing and promoting your novel is vital. And as an author you will be expected to assist in the publicity. It's likely you'll receive a marketing campaign if you've a book deal from a mainstream publisher. They will have a vested interest in your novel. Don't harass your publisher. You will not be the only author in their stable. You need to be ready to jump through hoops and over fences. The first-time writer with a modest advance is not guaranteed public attention but your publisher will endeavour to get your book reviewed or entered for prizes. However, the competition is as fierce as getting published in the first place. Pre-existing fame is useful for an author i.e. celebrity names have a ready-made readership. Word-of-mouth is good but it can take years to establish a readership. PANDORA

Marketing is essential especially if you're self-publishing. Be prepared to work hard to raise your profile as much as possible. Any ideas to market your book will be valuable.

marketing timelines

Marketing timelines are important to take into account when you're negotiating publicity and spreading information about your soon-to-be-published novel. As an author you will be expected to assist in the publicity or if you are self-publishing you will have to do it yourself. Be prepared to make yourself available for photos, interviews and to write promotional pieces about your novel. Magazines have long lead times—e.g. nine months. This is important if you're self-publishing and negotiating interviews and reviews for your novel. Newspapers have shorter lead times. Feature articles are planned a couple of months ahead. Local newspapers usually work on shorter times. Writing and producing online viral marketing takes long lead times. PANDORA

marketing tools [See also Book launch/Marketing/Talks]

Marketing tools such as posters, reviews, interviews, media appearances and using social media are all valuable. Short form copy, sound bites, tweets, taglines and headlines are useful to market your novel. Be prepared to describe your novel in 140 characters or less and have a list of snappy phrases and sound bites ready e.g. Sea change, beach read, accidental activist, high-rise development. Competitively priced, short e-books can be the perfect introductions to an author that readers may have missed. Slipping a chapter or two of a novel into the back of another novel can be a successful promotion as well as offering free copies of your novel online for a few days if you are on the e-publishing path. PANDORA

Start and think locally with your marketing; local newspapers, radio, TV station, bookshops, libraries et cetera.

mass-market novel [See also Commercial fiction]

A mass-market novel is a term that refers to a commercial or contemporary novel that appeals to a very large segment of the reading public. Mass-market novels are sold, frequently at discount prices, in outlets such as supermarkets, chain stores, as well as smaller bookstores and bookshops, and do really well selling online. PANDORA

McGuffin [See also Crime fiction/Whodunits]

McGuffin is a word for something that sets the action running in your novel. The writer only needs to impress on the minds of the reader that this thing (whatever it is) matters greatly to the characters and away goes the plot. A McGuffin is superfluous to the main plot. It's brushed aside once it has done its job of jump-starting the plot. The film director Alfred Hitchcock first gave the name McGuffin to an object—the plan, the formula, the microfilm—in his films, the spring that released the elaborate mechanism of his plots. VIOLET

meme

A meme is an idea, cultural style or action. It can spread from person to person on the Internet. LEE

merchandising rights [See also Contract]

Merchandising rights enable companies to create non-book products that spin-off from your novel. Your publisher or agent will negotiate these rights. If you're self-publishing you will have to do the negotiating. PANDORA

Members are negotiating writerly products *as spin-offs from this how-to guide. Hopefully the products e.g. quirky designer bags, notebooks, et cetera will bring in funds for Shelly Beach Community Centre & Library.*

metaphor [See also Imagery/Figure of speech/Simile]

A metaphor is a word or phrase that implies meaning through imagery. It's an implied comparison between two different things. For example: My life is an open book. Unlike a simile, a metaphor doesn't use *as* or *like*. Metaphors can work to create a character or add a sense of place. Sometimes a metaphor will appear at first try. Another time you will work very hard to find one. Mixed metaphors occur when inappropriate metaphors are used. For example: Digby's got his head in the sand and is leading the Action committee up the garden path. However, mixed metaphors can be used intentionally to create humour. GINA

Novelists do not get paid by the metaphor.

middle-chapter depression [See also Chapter/30,000 words]

Middle-chapter depression happens to many writers when they don't know how to fill the middle of their novel. They have a great beginning and end, but no middle. A solution can be to use the *cause-and-effect* technique to write your chapters. For example: something happens then something else must happen. It's like a domino effect. BILL

midnight scribblers

Midnight scribblers are a secret club of writers. It's possible to get your novel written using the Cinderella hours if you're a member of the Midnight Scribblers Club—those who are awake, and write at midnight and beyond. DAPHNE

mind mapping [See also Brainstorming]

Mind mapping is a technique that can help you plan ahead, and work out a solution for a writerly issue, plot, a scene, et cetera. It's usually the second stage of brainstorming. Take a blank sheet of paper, in the middle write the key word (i.e. character's name) or concept (i.e. the novel's theme *change*). From the word or concept draw lines and jot down keywords, phrases—anything that comes to your mind in free thinking. Keep branching off in tangents. Not all tangents will be useful but some will. Now start writing. GINA

mind your p's and q's

Mind your p's and q's is a phrase that relates to the early printing industry. It was a reminder to printers not to mix up these letters when putting them back in the rack after use. VIOLET

mise en scene [See also Setting/Scene]

Mise en scene is a French phrase for part of a scene in your novel. DIGBY

modifiers [See also Dangling modifier/Intensifiers]

Modifiers are words or phrases that weaken or soften the meaning of other words or phrases. For example: seem to, quite, tend to, hopefully, perhaps, almost, whatever. DIGBY

motivation [See also Characters/Flawed characters]

Motivation is what you need to write a novel. It's the drive to reach a goal. Motivation is also what makes your characters tick. They need to overcome obstacles to reach their goals. Motivation influences the decisions characters make and the directions they take in your plot. You can give your characters a range of motives and actions. You are writing fiction remember. However, your characters' motives should be believable. For example: don't have them charging off to the North Pole or falling down a well because you're sick of them. VIOLET

Make Motive Pages *to help sort your characters' actions in your plot. Use questions as headings to find out your characters' motives. What do they want? Why do they want it so badly? How do they intend to get it? What stops them getting it? How will they overcome the obstacle(s)?*

Ms [See also Submitting your novel]

Ms is the abbreviation for a manuscript. A manuscript was originally a handwritten copy. Now the word manuscript is used to describe a printed hard copy, a computer or file of a work i.e. your novel. DIGBY

Mss is the plural abbreviation.

multiple submissions

[See also Full submission/Partial/Submitting your novel]

Multiple submissions are copies of your novel sent simultaneously to different agents and publishers. Sending multiple submissions was a practice universally discouraged by editors in the past. Now it has gained acceptance. Writers should inform agents and publishers that the copy of their novel they're sending is a multiple submission. VIOLET

myth [See also Legend/Pandora's box]

A myth is a story about super humans or fictitious people in ancient times. Myths were traditionally used in the past to explain how natural phenomena or social customs came into being. DIGBY

N

NaNoWriMo [See also Camp NaNoWriMo]

NaNoWriMo is an abbreviation for National Novel Writing Month—an annual creative writing event run by a non-profit organisation to challenge authors to write a 50,000-word novel in a single month. It's held in the month of November and is a global initiative with over 200,000+ authors signing up to take part and write in a supportive online community of writers. JOSH

names [See also Characters/Pen name]

Names bring your characters to life. Use names appropriate to the culture, setting and time of your novel. For example: appropriate names for a historical novel, Italian names if you're setting your crime novel in the Mafia culture. Choose short names for your main character—you'll be keying this name frequently. Don't pick a name that's hard to read, pronounce or remember. Once you've named your main characters, choose supporting character names that sound different and begin with different letters to avoid confusing your reader. Books of names (e.g. *The Complete Book of Baby Names*) are handy reference tools to have on your bookshelf. VIOLET

Beware of giving a pet a ridiculously irritating name that will annoy readers.

narrative [See also Plot]

A narrative is writing that tells a story of events or experiences and has an ending. It can be factual or fictional, prose or poetry. DIGBY

nemesis

Nemesis is a word often mistakenly used to mean *an enemy,* a hostile person. However, nemesis is a much stronger word than enemy. Nemesis means an avenging force. In classical mythology *Nemesis* was the goddess of retribution. Today nemesis is used to mean an unbeatable rival or opponent. DIGBY

networking [See also F2F/Writers' Conferences/Writers' Groups]

Networking—mixing and talking F2F or online—with writers, book-industry people, and book lovers is invaluable when you're a writer. Writing is a solitary occupation. You need to get out into the world and meet other writers, especially if you wish to get your novel published. Using social networking (e.g. Twitter and Facebook) can equate to water-cooler time, cups-of-coffee or office-tea breaks to catch up on relevant *what's happening?* goss. GINA

non–exclusive rights

[See also Contract/DIY publishing/Hybrid author]

Non-Exclusive Rights occur when one edition of your novel is produced by a publisher, another edition can be produced in the same format, language or territory by another publisher. LEE

non-sequiturs

Non-sequiturs are irrelevant sentences that creep into your novel. They have no relation to the preceding sentence. They are easy to miss, have nothing to do with your plot, and you have no idea how they got there. BIANCA

Delete them.

notebook [See also Blog/Diary/Journal]

A notebook, paper or device, is equal to a writer's first-aid kit. You can use a notebook to record ideas, dreams, characters, plot points, dialogue and random-writer-thoughts for your novel. Don't wait until you own a designer pen and a moleskin-covered notebook with glace-icing paper. Any pocket notebook or device will do. Carry it with you at all times to avoid losing important stuff as you can do when you write notes on shopping dockets and serviettes. You only need a few choice, accurate words to prompt your memory when you return home. BIANCA

Don't use your notebook as an escape for not writing real stuff for your novel. And don't write in your notebook while people are talking to you. It's very off-putting for the non-writer.

noun [See also Grammar/Parts of speech/Verb]

A noun is the name for a person, place, thing and idea. There are different types of nouns. For example: abstract, collective, common, concrete, mass, proper and verbal nouns. If you're interested in grammar—or on the way to becoming a grammar buff—bone up on nouns in grammar books. DIGBY

novel [See also Fiction/Long fiction]

A novel is fictional writing and can come in many formats. For example: hard copy or digital. A novel usually contains about 300–700+ pages of words, phrases and sentences. Reading the 300–700 pages will hopefully give the reader many hours of pleasure and entertainment. DIGBY

novel outline [See also Chapter summary/Outline/Synopsis]

A novel outline or outline, is a chapter-by-chapter summary of a novel, frequently in paragraph form. It allows an agent or editor to evaluate the novel's content, tone and pacing to decide whether they want to see the entire manuscript for possible publication. BILL

novella [See also How long is a novel?]

A novella is a work of fiction that falls between a short story and a novel. Its length varies from 15,000 to 50,000 words. If you have an idea that is too complex for a short story but doesn't have the complexity for a novel it could be exactly right for a novella. A novella needs fully-fleshed characters and a plot that builds tension to a successful ending. It can be written around one or two—maybe more viewpoints and one or two conflicts—small or life changing. A novella's scope is not as vast as the novel or as limited as the short story. With the success of online publishing, novellas are in vogue and coming into their own as e-books. Novellas are a perfect way to reach a new readership and give your readers a taste of your writing style. DAPHNE

> *Don't get too caught up with the word count when you are writing. A novella will be as long as it needs to be.*

numbering pages

Numbering pages of your novel is a top priority for writers. Page numbers need to be easy to find and read. In a print book format, the number on the right-hand page called the recto—is always odd. The number on the left-hand page—called the verso—is always even. You can use features on software packages to automatically number the pages of your drafts. Never submit your novel to an agent or publisher without numbering your pages. You can never guarantee your novel will stay in one piece when it lands on a desk. VIOLET

Retrieving and assembling unnumbered pages of your novel—blown from the roof of your car or floating out to sea—can be a novelist's nightmare.

O

object [See also Predicate/Subject]

Object is a grammatical term used when explaining sentence structure. A basic sentence needs a subject—person or thing that is doing the action; and a verb—the action or event. If the sentence has something that is acted on by the subject and the action of the verb, it is called the object of the sentence. For example: **The Dog** [subject] **digs** [verb] **holes** [object]. DIGBY

Swot up on grammar books if you don't understand this explanation.

observing [See also Café writing/Listening/Notebook]

Observing, along with listening, are innate qualities in most writers. Observing human behaviour, interaction and the minutiae of everyday life, then transporting your observations into your novel, is an excellent way to make your novel believable. A writer can collect observations from just about anything. For example: newspapers, magazines, TV, films, overheard conversations et cetera. Keeping your observation antennae up will give you ideas, plot points, scenes, dialogue and characters to file away for future writing use. GINA

of/off

Of and *Off* are confusing words. *Of* is a preposition used to denote the possession or relationship between two things. *Off* can be used as an adverb to show when someone or something is away from a particular place or time, or as a preposition showing movement. For example: She was off with the fairies. VIOLET

of the

Of the are two small words that can slow the pace of your writing. Instead of using *of the*, use an adjectival or possessive approach to the noun. DIGBY

For example:

The cover of the *book.* ⌷x⌷   *The book cover.* ⌷√⌷

The owner of the *bookshop café.* ⌷x⌷ *The bookshop café owner.* ⌷√⌷

off the rack covers

[See also Book design/Book Design package/Cover designs]

Off the rack covers is a design term. The term refers to covers you buy on the Internet. Covers that will work as *place holders* i.e. covers with images that are OK for web use but are not print quality. *Off the rack covers* are cool to use for a soft launch followed by an official launch of your novel. LEE

O.K.

O.K.—also written as *ok* or *okay*—is a popular expression of agreement. It has a similar meaning to *cool* or *sweet.* JOSH

the one-point-five rule [See also Cushion deadline/Deadline]

The One-point-five Rule is useful for writers. Writers tend to underestimate how long it will take to complete their novel. Assume it will take one-and-a-half times longer than you estimate—then decide on your cushion deadline. BILL

online presence [See also Platform/Social media]

An online presence means having somewhere readers can find out about an author and an author's books on the Internet. Whether you are self-publishing or have a traditional publisher, a website, blog, and a presence on Facebook and Twitter sites, are expected by readers. Keeping your website, blog, Twitter and Facebook accounts updated is time consuming but it is expected by readers. BILL

Create a three-dimensional online presence. Not every post or tweet should be about you.

online slush pile

Online slush pile is a writerly term referring to the cyberspace pile your novel will land on when you digitally submit your novel to a publisher. Don't hold your breath for a rejection slip. Most publishers advise writers that if you don't hear from them in a certain number of weeks your novel is a *no go!* VIOLET

online storage [See also Cloud]

Online storage (storage for your computer files) is offered by various IT companies. The storage allows you to upload your files to their secure servers on the Internet. Your files can be easily accessed with a user name and password. If you're worried about uploading sensitive personal information online select a company that will encrypt your data so only you can access it. JOSH

> *You can make DIY online backups by sending your novel file to yourself and to writerly friends via email for safekeeping.*

online submission [See Submitting your novel]

onomatopoeia

Onomatopoeia is a term for words that suggest the sound they are describing for example: whizz, bang, crash, slosh, plop. BIANCA

out of print [See also Contract/Run]

Out of print (also written as o.p., OP or o/p) means your novel is no longer published. If your novel is o.p., you'll need to check your contract as to retaining copyright and placing your novel with another publisher or self-publishing. VIOLET

> *Keep in contact with your publisher's marketing department and keep track of your novel's print run.*

opening page [See also The first line/Opening paragraph]

An opening page must grip the reader and keep them reading the rest of your novel. VIOLET

> *Don't waste time writing that dynamic opening page. You can always rewrite it after you've completed your novel.*

opening paragraph [See also The first line/Paragraph]

The opening paragraph of a novel must keep a reader reading to the next paragraph, and the next, and the next. Imagine a potential buyer is reading your novel's first few paragraphs in a bookshop. If you've written too much unnecessary and boring information in your first few opening paragraphs, it could result in your novel being set aside for a zappier read. DAPHNE

organic [See also Characters]

Organic as used in the literary world describes writing—usually fictional characters—that are authentic. If the word organic is used to describe your novel it could mean the plot, setting and characters are believable. DAPHNE

orphan [See also Widow]

An orphan is a typesetting term for the first or last line of a paragraph that is standing alone at the top or bottom of a page. It looks odd and should be avoided. Some people use *widow* as a blanket term for undesirable short lines at the top or bottom of pages. VIOLET

Watch out for orphans and widows if you are self-publishing.

other reads [See also Beta Reader/Crit group/Feedback]

Other reads is a publishing term that refers to outside readers doing a trial read of your novel. Sometimes publishers employ *other reads* to get reactions and reviews of your novel before they decide to publish it. BILL

If you have a friend who is a Beta Reader and is prepared to be an other *read for you by reading the final draft of your novel treat them with care. They are few and far between.*

outline [See Chapter summary/Novel outline]

An outline is a simple, brief (dot-point even) breakdown of your novel. A few lines to describe scenes and chapters may be all that is needed. Think of an outline as a detailed table of contents. The length of your outline will depend on the length of your novel. BILL

oxymoron

An oxymoron is a phrase that contradicts itself. For example: creative non-fiction. DIGBY

over-writing

Over-writing is a writer's curse and to be avoided. Check your writing for over-the-top flowery, purple prose or ornate language. Watch out for an excess use of adjectives and adverbs, overuse of repetition and metaphors et cetera. DIGBY

over the transom [See also Proposal]

Over the transom is an old-fashioned phrase that describes the submission of an unsolicited manuscript. The term harks back to the time when mail—including writers' submissions—was delivered through the open window above a publisher's office door. VIOLET

P

pacing [See also Plot/Plot point/Scene]

Pacing is important in your novel. Action scenes increase the pace. Using writing techniques such as flashback, internal monologue, exposition and description can slow the pace. Pacing needs to follow the *Goldilocks* principle. It has to be just right. Think of your pacing as a rollercoaster ride. It starts slowly, rises to the top of a loop, then down again. Another slow stretch and it rises to the top of a loop again. To create pacing for suspense use short sentences and paragraphs. Cut everything that's not essential to pick up pace. LEE

padding [See also Novella/Subplot]

Padding can be the solution when you've completed the first draft of your novel and it's not long enough. Re-imagine your novel. Add a subplot or more to your plot. Expand on pivotal scenes, enlarge characters, add more descriptions et cetera. With the advent of online publishing a word count does not become the hidden dragon when you're writing your novel. LEE

If you're embarking on heavy padding (i.e. adding 30,000 words) watch you don't lose sight of your plot and bore your reader to death.

page 69

Page 69 is Marshall McLuhan's—a famous Canadian communicator's—theory about choosing a book. He said, *Open the book at Page 69 and read. If you like what you read, then buy it.* Obviously this will not work with all novels, as Page 69 could be a blank page, cover the most boring exposition or dialogue, or be a numberless e-book page.

Many readers judge a book by the cover, the back cover content or onscreen description before they decide to buy or borrow it. Other readers apply *the-first-page test* i.e. after reading the first page and liking it they will buy or borrow it. Some readers still use the five-finger test suggested by their fave children's librarian when they were younger. *Place a finger on every word you don't know. If your five fingers are used up on the first page—find another book to borrow.* DAPHNE

page-turner

A page-turner is a label for a novel filled with action, drama, suspense, romance, sex, excitement, blood and gore et cetera so the reader will keep turning the pages of your novel until they reach the last page. BIANCA

Pandora's Box [See also Metaphor/Myth]

Pandora's Box is a metaphor for a source of unknown troubles. In Greek mythology Zeus gave Pandora a casket containing all the ills of the world, which were released when Pandora opened the casket. Social media in its various forms can be a metaphor for Pandora's Box—a casket of messages. Messages and images when released into cyberspace can create unforeseen issues and consequences. PANDORA

panel copy [See also Spine/Strapline]

Panel copy refers to text on the front cover, spine and back cover (or dust jacket) of your novel. If a mainstream publisher publishes your novel, you may or may not be consulted or asked to contribute to the panel copy. However, if a small Indie publisher publishes your novel, you will probably work as a team. Obviously if you're self-publishing you will write the panel copy. Your panel copy should describe the premise and the spirit of your book in a concise, enticing way. LEE

Avoid being overly mysterious hoping you'll capture readers to read your novel when you write panel copy.

pantser [See also Plotter]

Pantser is a writerly word used to describe a writer's writing process. For example: He writes by the seat of his pants. A pantser follows their writerly intuition and develops their novel as they write it. Many successful best-selling authors use this method. BILL

paperback [See also e-book/Hardback/Self-publishing]

A paperback is the paper-covered format of a novel. Traditionally paperback formats were more convenient and cheaper than a hardback copy of the same novel. They usually came out many months later than the hardback copy. Many dog-eared and battered paperbacks are still much-loved treasures for readers. Today digital publishing is changing the timing of a novel's release. An e-book format may be the first edition of a novel, combining with a paperback release later and skipping the publication of the hardback copy completely. PANDORA

It's all about pricing, sales and marketing.

paragraph [See also Sentence]

A paragraph is one or more sentences used to develop and explore an idea or action. Avoid a series of one-sentence paragraphs. Vary the sentence lengths. A traditional paragraph should have a beginning, middle and an end. Usually the first sentence introduces the topic then other sentences follow to develop the topic. A paragraph should not contain one unnecessary sentence. Start a new paragraph when there is a new idea or action. VIOLET

There's nothing harder to read than a paragraph-less page. Learn how to write paragraphs if you're unsure how to use them effectively.

parentheses [See Brackets]

partial [See also Submitting your novel/Query]

A partial is the first five pages of your novel—a taster to be read and evaluated by agents, publishers, editors and writerly friends. BILL

participles [See also Dangling modifier/Verb]

Participles are forms of verbs. Every verb has two participles—a present participle and a past participle. Regular verbs are verbs that use *ed, d, en, n or t* to form the past participle, and *ing* to form the present participle.

Verb	Past participle	Present participle
dance	danced	dancing
write	written	writing

Irregular verbs such as *dig* and *swim* form the past participle in a different way.

Verb	Past participle	Present participle
dig	dug	digging
swim	swum	swimming

Participles can act as adjectives. It is important not to let past participles dangle. They need to be linked with the right word. DIGBY

For example:

We could see the pelicans flying overhead. [√]

Flying overhead, we could see the pelicans. [x]

parts of speech [See also Grammar]

Parts of speech have special parts to play in the structure of a sentence. There are eight parts of speech in the English language: adjectives, adverbs, conjunctions, interjections, nouns, prepositions, pronouns, and verbs. DIGBY

passive voice [See also Active voice]

Passive voice is a grammatical term. Writing that has a passive voice has passive verbs and sentences where the subject is acted upon. The word *by* frequently indicates passive voice. For example: The writer was bitten *by* the dog. The plot was lost *by* Lee. Passive voice creates distance between the character(s) and the reader. It makes the reader an observer rather than a participant. GINA

Avoid the passive voice in your writing. It's less direct and harder to read. Go for Active voice. (Not all SBWG members agree with this tip!)

the pay-off [See also Plot]

The Pay-off is a phrase used by writers to describe the ending of their novel. It's an ending that wraps up the plot for their reader. BILL

> *Many novels don't have a* pay-off *ending. The reader is left to make up his or her own ending. This can be cool.*

PDF [See also POD]

PDF is an abbreviation for Portable Document Format commonly created in *Adobe Acrobat.* PDF refers to an electronic version of a file that can be printed as a hard copy. These files are locked so that you can't amend the text, however *Adobe Acrobat* has tools that enable you to write corrections to the file. LEE

pen name [See also Anon/Choosing a Pen Name]

A pen name is a name a writer chooses to use when they write. A pen name, also called pseudonym and *non de plume*, is a false or extra name an author uses instead of their legal name. Pseudonym is Greek for *false name*, and *nom de plume* is French for *name of pen.* An author may use a pen name or pseudonym as a means of disguise. For example: they don't want to be outed as a writer of erotic fiction. In the past, using a pen name was a convenient transgender device for female writers. For example: George Eliot (Mary Ann Evans), Currer, Ellis and Acton Bell (Charlotte, Emily and Ann Bronte) chose masculine names in order to sell their novels. Ironically in today's publishing industry male writers use female pen names. VIOLET

perfect binding

Perfect binding is a form of book binding in which signatures of pages—pages that are collected and folded in groups of four, eight or 16—are cut and glued together to form a spine. VIOLET

permission [See also Epigraph/Quotes]

Permission is a publishing term. You or your publisher can grant permission to people who want to quote from your novel. People usually pay a fee for the right to quote from your novel. You will need to clear *permission* for any copyrighted material you quote in your novel, such as an epigraph. BILL

phishings [See also Backup]

Phishings are email scams that rely on tricking screen readers into clicking on a web link. Writers should be aware of these scams when they're trawling the net instead of writing *the* novel. The purpose of phishing is to deceive users into voluntarily giving their personal details such as bank login details. VIOLET

Install protection software on your computer.

a Phoenix novel [See also Branding/Marketing]

A Phoenix novel is similar to a Phoenix company that collapses one day with a pile of debt and rises from the ashes like the bird in Greek mythology—same assets, slightly different name. Fraudulent practices enable the Phoenix company to avoid taxes, wages and other bills. Ignoring the fraudulent practices bit, published and unpublished writers can rewrite and rebrand their novels—make them rise from the ashes—pitch and launch them into cyberspace via self-publishing. PANDORA

photographs [See also Branding/Marketing]

Photographs of yourself—head and shoulders portrait, with your pet, in your writing place, balancing on the end of a windy pier or standing on the edge of a cliff-top et cetera are necessary for publicity when you become a novelist. A photo shoot can be nerve wracking. Have your hair and/or make-up professionally styled. It'll help you feel cool and boost your confidence for a studio shoot, or when a professional photographer comes to your house. In the past *back cover* photographs of authors were taken in their salad days i.e. when they were younger. Up-to-date photographs are required for publicity shots today. However with many published authors discovering their backlists for e-publishing, it's quite cool for an author to find a younger photograph of themselves to promote their children's books or novels published years ago PANDORA

Always have publicity photographs you like on hand. You'll hate the photographs taken by a hungry in-house photographer who can't wait to take your photo and race off to grab a pie for lunch.

phrase [See also Grammar]

A phrase is a group of words that has a meaning within a sentence, but doesn't make a complete sentence by itself. For example: on Shelly Beach, at Piece-of Cake bookshop café, the eight writing group members. There are different kinds of phrases such as adjectival, adverbial, and prepositional phrases. DIGBY

piece

A piece is a writerly word to refer to an article you write for a journal or magazine hopefully to promote your novel. DIGBY

piggybacking [See also Marketing]

Piggybacking is a useful strategy when marketing your novel. When there's a popular story or novel there's always room for another similar novel. Use the piggybacking principle and take advantage of opportunities to write articles or posts on the theme or contents of your novel. Send a press release to the media. PANDORA

Pinterest [See also Social media]

Pinterest is a popular social media site with millions of users. It enables people to share images, videos, hobbies et cetera on a virtual pin board. It can be a useful social media for authors to promote their books. BIANCA

pitch [See also Elevator pitch/Logline/Marketing]

A pitch is a presentation to sell your novel to an agent or a publisher. A pitch is usually delivered in a few moments of time. You can make a verbal, written or online pitch. Some verbal pitches are alarmingly short. For example: a 30-second pitch, a 90-second pitch, and a 3-minute elevator pitch. Written pitches can also be short and pithy. They can be written as short or long (10, 25, 50 or 100 word) sentences to describe your novel, a five-and ten-catch-word pitch, and a two-sentence pitch. Transfer your pitch into short-form copy and sound bites, tweets, headlines and taglines. Sprinkle keywords and headline-ready phrases throughout your online book description. These sound bites will be the ones that publishing insiders and readers will remember and share. PANDORA

Practise repeating your pitch aloud so you are prepared when anyone asks. What's your novel about? *Be ready to sell your novel at any time.*

plagiarism [See also Copyright/Ideas]

Plagiarism is taking another writer's work and passing it off as your own. It's copying a certain quantity of text, word-for-word, or as near to it so it doesn't make a difference. Plagiarism includes but is not the same as infringing copyright. Copyright covers specific use of material. If you're a victim of plagiarism you can sue in civil courts for loss of earnings and reputation. However, plagiarism is costly to prove in terms of finances—lawyers' fees are huge—time and stress. Some famous authors have been taken to the civil courts for plagiarism but with little success. Plagiarism does happen—but rarely. Enjoy trialling your writing in a secure writers' network. BILL

Remember there is no copyright on ideas or titles. To avoid being an unwitting plagiariser, catalogue your reference material sources. Sometimes you may feel your writing is so brilliant it can't be yours. Google to make sure it is yours.

plan [See also Grasshopper writer/Outline]

A plan is a useful thing to have if you're writing a novel. Some writers like to meticulously plan their novel before they start writing. Others enjoy winging it. Go with whatever works for you. You don't necessarily have to follow your plan, but it will be there to fall back on if you need it. GINA

Some novels write themselves without a plan.

plane book [See also Airport novel]

A Plane book in readerly terms is not a book about airplanes—but it could be. The term refers to a novel you select to read on a plane during a long flight. You need to apply the Goldilocks theory to your selection. A *plane book* needs to be just right—not too long or too short. A novel of 700+ pages could be too long, and too heavy if you pack the hard copy edition in your cabin luggage. However, if a *plane book* is under 200 pages you could finish it before you reach your destination. Crime novels are good – but not if the plot is too complicated, and you nap, and can't remember where you were up too. BIANCA

> *Take a selection of e-books on your e-reader. Otherwise take old paperbacks and leave them behind for other readers at an airport terminal.*

platform [See also Author platform/Branding/Marketing]

Platform is a marketing word. It refers to the star quality and background experience an author brings with their novel. Publishers look for an author with a platform to promote the sale of a novel. For example: a photogenic, verbally competent and highly intelligent pole-dancer will have an excellent platform to support the sale of her novel, *The Pole-Dance Murders.* PANDORA

plot [See Genre/Plotter/Subplots]

Plot is an essential element in a novel. A plot is like a map or blueprint of your novel. It's what characters do to overcome problems or conflict in their lives, and how they move to a resolution. A basic plot should have a beginning, a middle where things happen, and a satisfactory ending. Plots are determined by the conventions of the genre of the novel you're writing. For example: a detective must always get the criminal in crime fiction, the girl usually gets the boy or vice versa, et cetera in romantic fiction. Every plot needs complications. Complications are not situations—they're events that happen.

Complications or conflict must cause characters to change and to make choices. **BILL**

plot line [See also Plot]

A plot line is the line of events that are written in your plot. It's a useful tool to draw up and use for planning, revising and rewriting your novel. **BILL**

plot point [See also Plot]

A plot point is an event in your novel—a dramatic development that moves the action on and changes your novel. For example: The dog gets lost. **GINA**

plot twist

A plot twist is a literary device used to keep your readers enthralled and turning the pages of your novel. Written well it can create a *Wow! I never saw that coming!* reaction. For example *Jane Eyre* had no idea who was in the attic and Pip had the wrong idea about the identity of his benefactor in *Great Expectations*. Agatha Christie was a master at using plot twists. Contemporary authors such as the best-selling novelist Jody Piccoult use plot twists brilliantly. A classic example of a plot twist in the very last pages is Scott Turow's procedural crime fiction *Presumed Innocent*. **DIGBY**

To create a plot twist in your novel, brainstorm alternative endings, choose the best and work that into your original plot as the twist. Caution: written badly a plot twist can cause readers to hate your novel.

plotter [See also Pantser]

Plotter is a word used by writers to describe their writing process. A plotter plots, plans and organises their novel before they begin the first draft. Some writers can take years developing this process before they start writing their novel. BIANCA

plu-perfect [See also Had/Flashback/Verb]

Plu-perfect is a grammatical term for the past perfect use of a verb. You add *had* to the past perfect form of the verb e.g. *written, talked, walked.* For example: She *had written* her novel five years ago. He *had talked* with his ex-wife before he killed her. They *had walked* to the end of the pier and back. The plu-perfect tense is used to refer to events that happen prior to an already past action. You identify plu-perfect tense by the use of the word *had.*

Use the plu-perfect tense when you step in and out of a flashback.

POD [See also Self–publishing]

POD is the abbreviation for print-on-demand. POD is a production process that enables you, or a publisher you have employed, to print small numbers of hard copies of your novel. Be realistic. If your novel has bestseller potential go for it. If not—then aim to sell the first 100 copies and celebrate when you do. PANDORA

Make sure you don't end up with huge numbers of your novel packed in every corner of your home, garage, et cetera.

Pop-Up Writing Event [See also Writers' Groups]

A Pop-Up Writing Event is a one-time function. Hold a Pop-Up Writing Event if you've credentials as a presenter—or you can engage a presenter with credentials—or you have a room or an outside area that will take at least eight people. You can also hold a workshop on a specific theme, a writerly Q&A session or invite an editor or published writer as speaker. Decide on a time—day or night—and offer simple refreshments such as coffee, tea and biscuits. You can charge admittance, provide a free event or charge and donate the funds to a local charity. DAPHNE

Members suggest it helps to have a flexible personality if you hold Pop-Up Events. Keep records of attendees so you have a subscriber list. You may have enough takers to start a writers' group.

Pop-Up Writing Group Venue

A Pop-Up Writing Group Venue is useful if the members of your writers' group need somewhere quiet to write. Check with members who have a room that would be suitable, and times when members can use the Pop-Up Writing Venue. There should be no ties or interruptions for the writer using the Pop-Up Venue. However, the members providing the venue may like to provide a DIY cup of tea or coffee. DAPHNE

A Writing Group member will need to make a roster for members using the Pop-Up Venue and keep it up-to-date.

popular novels [See Commercial fiction]

portmanteau words [See also Word]

Portmanteau words are blended words such as brunch, (breakfast + lunch), smog (smoke + fog), blog (web + log). Lewis Carroll created the word portmanteau to describe the nonsense words he invented in his poem *Jabberwocky*. *Portmanteau* is a French word for a suitcase that has two separate compartments in it. DIGBY

POS [See also Bookshops/Marketing]

POS is the abbreviation for point-of-sale. A POS is the counter or sales area in a retail shop. Promotion material for books such as competitions, bookmarks, flyers, book club notes, catalogues et cetera are sent to bookshops by publishers to be used at the point-of-sale. PANDORA

If you're a hybrid author you can ask your local bookshop, store or library to distribute material to promote your book at their POS.

post-it notes

Post-it notes, and their cousins, post-it tape flags are useful for writers. Use post-it notes for quick notes about your novel, reminders, and to mark pages of your drafts et cetera. Use colour-coded post-it tape flags to mark divisions in your novel, research material, and text needing revision et cetera. BIANCA

Stick post-it notes all over your house to remind you to Just write!

postlims

Postlims are padding; pages containing advertisements for other novels, at the end of a novel. VIOLET

POV [See Characters]

POV, also called point-of-view and viewpoint, is the voice and view of the narrator of the story in your novel. A writer can choose to use first person, third person, an omniscient narrator or multiple points-of-view. These are terms describing the use of *I*, *you*, or *he/she* in your writing. First person POV is when the main character is telling the story using *I*. Second person POV addresses a *you* that can be the reader of your story. Third person POV tells the story by another person's viewpoint. It's a fly-on-the-wall viewpoint. The narrator uses pronouns *she* and *he*. The omniscient narrator POV uses *he* or *she*, knows everything about the characters in the novel and may—or may not—reveal everything. The omniscient narrator is unknown to characters in the novel. This viewpoint is often referred to as a Godlike viewpoint. A writer can also use multiple narrators to tell the story from different characters' points-of-view.

point-of-view [See POV]

practice/practise

Practice and Practise are two words that often confuse writers. Practice is a noun. It means the application of the use of a plan. For example: A dental practice. *Practise* (with an *s*) is a verb. It means *to rehearse, to do something over and over*. For example: Bianca had to practise reading aloud for her guest-author visit. If you're writing a novel for the US market, the word practise is used as both the noun and the verb. BIANCA

Ice *is a noun. Practice spelt with* ice *is the noun.*

predicate [See also Grammar/Object/Subject]

The predicate is a grammatical term. It's the part of a sentence that says something about the subject. In a sentence it is made up of the verb plus an object. For example: The cat *caught the mouse.* DIGBY

preface

Preface is an introduction to a book, usually explaining the content or intention of the book. Commercial novels are usually devoid of prefaces. BILL

prefix [See also Suffix]

A prefix is a group of letters at the beginning of a word, or word stem that add to, or change the word's meaning. For example: sub + plot = subplot.

prelims [See also Acknowledgements/Dedication/Front matter]

Prelims is the abbreviation for preliminary pages, and is a publishing term for the pages that occur before the start of your novel. For example: the copyright page, title page, dedication and acknowledgements et cetera. VIOLET

premise [See also Elevator pitch/Logline]

A premise is the sales tool, the calling card for your novel. It's a statement of character and conflict. Knowing the premise of your novel can help you keep sharper focus through the process of writing a novel. BILL

> *To get started you need to write a 2 or 3 word description of the main character's wants [goal] because [motivation] but [conflict].*

preposition [See also Grammar/Noun/Pronoun]

A preposition is a word that shows the relation between the object and some other word in the sentence. Prepositions are followed by a noun or pronoun in a sentence and relate to another. For example: The Dog sleeps *on* the bed. The suitcase is *under* the bed. Gina is *in* the bed. According to the old school of grammar, a preposition should not be used at the end of a sentence. However today it's acceptable to end a sentence with a preposition as long as the writer's meaning is clear. GINA

press release [See also Marketing/Photograph]

A press release is a one-page announcement sent to the media to promote your novel. It has a standard format (headline, story, quotes, contact information). Hopefully the whole release will be used or it will prompt publicists and journalists to get in touch, interview you or commission a different feature of their own about your novel.

Think about good stories connected to you or your writing. Include different information from what you presented in your back copy for your novel, blurb or your website. Consider these questions: How did you come to choose the subject or theme of your novel? What professional expertise qualifies you to write your novel? (Always write about your achievements in the third person.) Where do you live? (Only if this is significant to your novel.) And include an interesting photograph. What have others said about you? (Include some quotes.) Is the subject matter of your novel topical? If so provide a link to relevant coverage and offer a journalist a ready-made issue-based piece with your novel as supporting proof. PANDORA

Beware of offering sensational information about yourself. You'll have to live with it forever. And don't link your novel to something newsworthy if you don't feel ready to comment on it or have your novel linked with it in the future.

primary research

[See also Historical fiction/Research/Secondary research]

Primary research, sometimes called empirical research, is a term for research based on first-hand experience. For example: an interview, a diary, a journal, eye-witness accounts, speeches or statistics. DIGBY

print book [See also e-book]

A print book, also called a paper book refers to what was universally known as a *book* until digital or e-books came into being. Young children frequently refer to print books as *tree* books. VIOLET

Members recommend you indulge yourself and read a print book. Value the smell and the feel of the pages.

procrastination [See also Writers' Block]

Procrastination happens while you're waiting for the gold fish to die before you start your novel. Or when you must have the cleanest desk, kitchen, home, whatever, before you can sit down to write. Put your notes to one side, in a box in a bottom drawer or in a file on the computer. Write every day, even if it is one paragraph. Draft without stopping to edit. You can rewrite later. To avoid procrastinating when researching set a time for research, or put a limit on the sources you'll use. Stay on-task and focused, especially when researching online. DAPHNE

Some writers put glue on their chair before they sit down to write.

prologue [See also Protagonist/Thriller]

A prologue is a section of writing that comes before your actual story. If you're writing a thriller, a prologue can show your protagonist escaping from a harrowing predicament—think James Bond. You can continue your protagonist's story in Chapter One. LEE

pronoun [See also Grammar/Parts of speech]

A pronoun is a word that replaces a noun. There are personal pronouns (e.g. I, me, we and us), and pronouns used in dialogue to others (e.g. you and yourself). *Who, what* and *whose* are pronouns used in asking questions. DIGBY

proof [See also Galley/Proofreader]

A proof is the reproduction of a typeset page for the purpose of correction or checking. As the author you will be required to check errors, and make corrections. You will also be required to give approval and sign proofs off. Today most hard copy proofs are emailed as digital copies. VIOLET

Check with your editor if you find any proof-editing issues, queries about the layout and conformity with the house style sheet.

proofing [See also Proofreader]

Proofing is a term used to describe the period when the author has received, and is reviewing the typeset pages. BILL

proofreader [See also Editor]

A proofreader is absolutely focused on making corrections on the text of your novel when it has been typeset. That is after your novel has been copy edited, designed and is a nearly finished product. A proofreader searches for any typos and makes sure that all the copy editor's notes and edits have been implemented. Proofreaders also check page numbers, the copyright page and other copy or styling changes introduced during the production process. BILL

A proofreader doesn't look to do any big picture *editing i.e. moving chapters, cutting unnecessary paragraphs, rewriting sentences or make any other changes that could introduce new errors at this stage.*

proofreading [See also Editing/Proof]

Proofreading is the final stage of editing by a proofreader (or an editor) to ensure your novel is error-free before a mainstream or indie publisher publishes it. Proofreading involves checking page proofs, the typeset version of your novel. The proofreader will check that all text and images are accurately and consistently typeset. They will also check the structural and copy editing issues. As the author you will be sent the final proofs. Only minor changes should be made at this stage. Major changes can affect pagination and can be costly. BILL

Members cannot stress enough that if you are self-publishing, your novel will need to be edited and/or proofread. Employ people to do it to maintain objectivity.

proposal [See also Cover letter/Pitch/Query letter]

A proposal for a novel consists of a cover letter, a synopsis and sample—about ten per cent—of the finished novel, three chapters usually in order, or the first 50 pages to send to an agent or publisher. You may also need an author biography. VIOLET

What you send is determined by what the agent or publisher requests.

protagonist [See also Antagonist/Characters]

A protagonist is a writerly word for the leading or chief character—not the supporting character—in your novel. The prefix is derived from the Greek *protos*, meaning *first*, and *agonistes* a contender for a prize. A protagonist can be a hero or anti-hero. DIGBY

Do not use protagonist as plural as there can be only one protagonist in any novel. Do not qualify protagonist with chief or leading as the word already contains these meanings.

protecting your novel [See also Backup/Contract/Plagiarism]

Protecting your novel is mandatory practice for a writer. Always keep electronic backups and a hard copy of your novel. Send a SSAE to ensure your manuscript will be returned if you're submitting a hard copy to a mainstream publisher. Protect your novel from plagiarism by writing the copyright symbol © and your name at the end of your novel. When a publisher accepts your novel they will ask you to sign a contract. It is important you have this contract checked. VIOLET

Be alert. Disastrous things can happen to a publishing company that has your novel. The publishing company (together with your much-loved editor) may vanish into cyberspace and so can your novel.

pseudonym [See Choosing a Pen Name/Pen name]

public domain

Public domain is when published works are available for use without permission because they were never copyrighted, or because the copyright term has expired. It is the life of the author plus 70 years before a published work falls into public domain. BILL

SBWG members advise you to check before you use a work without permission.

publishing right [See also Contract]

A publishing right is the right someone has to publish your novel in print and digital form. Sometimes the print and digital editions are sold separately, but in mainstream publishing this is becoming less common. Publishers traditionally buy rights from an author to publish their novel. Agreement will be made on what formats and which territories and languages the publisher is buying the rights for. If you're self-publishing you control your publishing rights. JOSH

publishing services

[See also DIY publishing/Hybrid author/Self-publishing]

Publishing services can assist writers to self-publish their novels—including editing, formatting, printing, cover and book designing, distribution, sales, marketing et cetera—as a print or e-book. VIOLET

pun [See also Homonyms]

A pun is a humorous play on a word. A pun needs a word that has the same or similar sound, but different meaning or spelling. Puns are often used for titles of novels. For example: The Dog's Tale. VIOLET

punctuation

[See also Grammar/Grammar Check/The Greengrocer's apostrophe]

Punctuation is a system of symbols added to written words to show meaning, and make it easier for the reader to read your novel. Punctuation is not a pernickety set of rules designed to trip up the unwary. It was invented to help people read aloud. A few hundred years ago *not* many people could read, so those who could, read to those who couldn't. Points were added to pages to indicate to readers when to take a breath and what to emphasise. Today you can use a comma to show a short pause, a colon to show a medium-sized pause and a full stop to show a long pause. BIANCA

Writers and other people spend a huge amount of time arguing about punctuation. The use of punctuation in your novel can depend on your individual choice or the house style of your publisher. Some best-selling novels have been written with minimum punctuation or minus punctuation completely.

Q

QL [See Query]

quels [See also Fanfic/Fantasy fiction/Speculative fiction]

Quels is a writerly word used for prequels, sequels, mid-quels and squeakuels.

A squeakuel is when you're writing a follow-up for your novel written about animal characters that squeak. Quels usually refer to books in a series of a novel. Writers and fans of science fiction or speculative fiction will be familiar with quels. Quels can stand alone as novels and can be written in any order.

A sequel can be a follow-up to your original novel. A prequel can fill in plot points or stories of your main characters before they appeared in your original novel. A mid-quel can be a second novel taking place between two points in your original novel. It can tell the story of a character crucial to your plot.

Some published authors write quels for well-known literary novels e.g. *Pride and Prejudice*. VIOLET

If you're pitching quels to agents or publishers begin...
The second (third, fourth, whatever) book takes place...

qwerty keyboard [See also Typewriter]

The Qwerty keyboard is an inefficient and ergonomically unsound—your left hand does well over half the work—keyboard layout that is still going strong after 140 years. It was first produced in 1873; first on clunky mechanical typewriters, then with electronic word processors and computers. The Qwerty keyboard has survived for the simple reason that it got there first. The big lesson of Qwerty was the fact that it was standard. To any writer who *touch types* or *hunts-and-pecks*, using the Qwerty keyboard is as automatic as handwriting. Despite its myriad of faults it is hardwired into an author's brain. BILL

query [See also Cover letter]

A query (also known as a QL or a cover letter) is a business email or letter, usually no longer than a page, in which you sell your novel to an agent or publisher. It's your one-shot chance to be noticed by an agent or a publisher. Imagine you have less than a minute to capture an agent's or editor's attention and interest. A query should include a quick engaging explanation of your novel, its market and your credentials. Be straightforward. Agents and editors want a visible idea, a clear market and a writer with credibility and marketing savvy. BILL

Don't send your complete manuscript to an agent or publisher who specifies first *approach by query letter* or *query letter only in first instance.*

quest [See also Fantasy fiction/Speculative fiction]

A quest as featured in legends, is used as the structure or plot driver in fantasy or speculative fiction, and many forms of commercial novels. The quest legend is when the heroine (or hero) goes through a cycle of adventures, searches and journeys. They eventually reach—or fail to reach—their goal. For example: a silver cup or a miraculous object with healing powers. JOSH

question mark (?) [See also Punctuation]

A question mark (?) is a punctuation mark used at the end of sentences that ask a question. The question mark is sometimes used with other punctuation marks such as brackets, ellipsis, and quotation marks. A question mark is not needed with indirect questions. DIGBY

questions to ask about your plot [See also Plot]

Questions to ask about your plot can include:

1. Is your story believable? Have you suspended disbelief for your reader? (Coleridge) The world or universe of your novel must make sense for the reader.

2. Does your plot fit within the genre or subdivision of your novel i.e. *crime fiction* or *cosy crime fiction?*

3. Is the conflict for your protagonist—main character—strong enough and does it escalate?

4. Are solutions to an obstacle too easily overcome?

5. Have you delayed the plot unnecessarily? JOSH

quick grammar check [See also Grammar]

* **Noun:** naming word e.g. *dog, Gina*
* **Pronoun:** refers back to a previously mentioned noun e.g. *he, she, it, they.*
* **Verb:** a doing or action word. e.g. *digging, twirling, squealing.*
* **Adverb:** modifies a verb or an adjective e.g. *very.*
* **Adjective:** modifies or describes a noun e.g. *The reluctant writer.*

* **Preposition:** links parts of sentences together, and/or describes relationships e.g. *The dog who was owned by Gina dodged the dog catcher.*
* **Conjunction:** joins words, phrases and clauses e.g. *The dog and the cat.*
* **Interjection:** Adds emotion to a sentence e.g. *Your novel topped the bestseller list?* Stands alone from a sentence e.g. *Wow!* BIANCA

quintology [See also Series]

A quintology is a five-novel series. Some writers plan to write and gain a contract with a proposal for a five-novel series. JOSH

quotation marks (' ' and " ")

[See also Direct Speech/Quotations within quotations/Speech marks]

Quotation marks (' ' and " "), also called *speech marks,* are used to punctuate words that are spoken—dialogue, or direct speech. They always operate in pairs. When you begin with quotation marks, you must also close with quotation marks. Quotation marks are sometimes called inverted commas, because the beginning mark is an upside-down comma. There are single ' ' quotation and double " " quotation marks. Some writers like to use double quotation marks (" ") other writers use single quotation marks (' ') in their writing. Quotation marks can also be used to point a name, an invented word, quotations, quotations within quotations and special words. Publishers follow their own house style when they publish novels. DIGBY

Some publishers, and countries prefer to use double quotation marks, others single. Single quotation marks are less fussy, both to look at and to write. If you are self-publishing it doesn't matter which quotation marks you use in your novel as long as you are consistent.

quotations within quotations

[See also Direct Speech/Quotation marks/Quote]

Quotations within quotations occur when an excerpt from a book or person is quoted within another quotation. The quotation inside the main quotation is placed in marks of its own. If single quotation marks are used for the main quotation, double marks are used for the second quotation or vice versa. This helps to separate the two quotations. In the US double quotation marks are used for the main quotation and single marks for the second quotation. In the United Kingdom, single quotation marks are more often used for the main quotation and double marks for the second quotation. In countries like Australia, New Zealand, Canada both methods are used. DIGBY

quote [See also Dialogue/Punctuation/Quotation marks]

A quote or a quotation is a written or spoken passage repeated exactly in another publication, speech or conversation with an acknowledgement of its source. VIOLET

Check you have the correct quote and its source.

R

radio and TV reading [See also Contract/Publishing right]

Radio and TV reading—a straight reading from your novel for radio and TV—is different from a dramatisation and the rights can be sold separately. Your publisher or agent can negotiate this fee. If you're self-publishing you will need to negotiate the fees. PANDORA

a random-matter-of-fact ending [See also HEA]

A random-matter-of-fact ending will not satisfy your readers if you're writing a specific genre i.e. romantic or crime fiction. For example: a detective should not appear on the last few pages and solve the crime but maybe your romance genre doesn't need a HEA (happy-ever-after) ending. GINA

read [See also Book club/Radio and TV reading]

Read recent debut and bestselling novels published by major and other publishers—print and e-books. Particularly read critically acclaimed and best-selling novels in the genre you're writing. This will help you understand what your readers want and expect from your novel. Be a careful and voracious reader. Observe and practise writing techniques other novelists use. You need to understand how novels work. BILL

The more you read the better you'll write.

real-time scene [See also Chapter/Interior monologue/Scene]

A real-time scene is a literary phrase to refer to a dramatic scene that propels your novel. A real-time scene enables your character to act and move your plot forward. Real-time scenes have a beginning, middle and an ending. The beginning introduces the setting, the characters, their connection and behaviour. The middle section develops the conflict. The end of a real-time scene sees the character(s) make decisions to resolve the conflict. BILL

real-time stuff

Real-time stuff—using real names of people, businesses and organisations in your novel is cool but be careful you don't defame anyone. Most of the time people, organisations and companies will be happy to see their names, brands or products mentioned in your novel. If you've mentioned real-time stuff it's a good idea to notify people, organisations, businesses et cetera before your novel is published. For example: the owners of a company may object to their company building being the setting for gruesome serial murders in your novel. Go for a fictional company name. BIANCA

recycling-bin writing [See also Freelance writing]

Recycling-bin writing is collecting discarded sentences, paragraphs, scenes, characters, chapters, pages et cetera from your novel and reworking them. Use them as starting points, or shape them into feature articles or short stories to promote your novel. DAPHNE

Discarded ideas, subplots or characters frequently become the seeds for other novels.

red herring [See also Crime fiction/Too many red herrings/Whodunits]

A red herring is a writerly term for a well-planned and planted false clue in whodunits or crime fiction. Red herrings—small or large—used in crime fiction make for engrossing detective plots. VIOLET

red pen [See also Blue pen/Proof/Track Changes]

A red pen is traditionally used in the publishing process by proofreaders for all typesetting errors. A blue pen is traditionally used for an author and editor's corrections and changes, and a pencil for queries. VIOLET

redundant

Redundant is a writerly word to describe the unnecessary repletion of a word. For example: *free* gift, *close* proximity, *return* back, stand *up* and sit *down*. DIGBY

references books [See Writers' Tools]

rejection [See also Feedback/Reviews/Submitting your novel]

Rejection is part of the professional writing process. It can have positive as well as negative outcomes for writers. In order to cope with rejection, a writer needs to develop the thick skin of a hippopotamus or a rhinoceros. On the positive side, rejection can inspire you to improve your writing skills and consequently your novel. Re-evaluate your writing after a rejection. Rewrite or stand by what you've written. Send it out again. If you're a DIY publisher you'll not have to worry about rejections. Then again, online reviews can be dodgy and hurtful and you'll probably feel rejected if your sales numbers are low. BIANCA

The easiest way to avoid rejection is not to send your novel to an agent or publisher or to send it without your name and address.

rejection letter/slip or email [See also Submitting your novel]

A rejection letter/slip, or email are ways in which an agent or publisher indicates they're not interested in your novel. Don't bin the rejection straight away! Sometimes an agent or editor will write encouraging and helpful comments. They may even say they'd be interested in reading your novel again—if you do a rewrite. It's up to you. Sometimes an editor, agent or publisher has been known to change their mind and accept your submission. Keep copies of your rejection letters, slips and emails. File them. When you become a best-selling author they can make entertaining copy for presentations at writers' festivals and events. BILL

In the past, hugely successful authors were known to wallpaper their rooms with rejection slips. In the future, authors will have to store their rejection emails in cyberspace.

reminders [See also Cover letter/Online submission/Query]

Reminders are polite notes, phone or email queries you can use to communicate with agents or publishers if they're taking a huge amount of time to get back to you re a phone call, cover letter, or email query regarding an answer to your submission or royalty payments due to you. PANDORA

research [See also Facts/Factoids/Historical fiction/Tools of the trade]

Research is important when writing most novels. Research can make a novel credible—especially historical fiction. You need to research to write an authentic account of the time and setting of your novel for your readers. Research can come before, while you write, or after writing a first draft for your novel. When you include a fact in your novel (e.g. the length of a man-eating shark) double-check. If in doubt cut it out or replace it with another fact e.g. a giant squid of an indeterminate length. Libraries and the Internet via Google searches are great resources to research dates, countries, places, culture, background et cetera for your novel. Interviewing people i.e. a forensic scientist or a police person can help you with research on occupations or ways of poisoning a victim. Research also means doing *real* stuff. For example: travelling on a local bus to get the feel and ambiance of being a local bus traveller. BIANCA

If you don't like researching, learn to like it until your novel becomes a bestseller and you're rich and famous. Then you can employ a research assistant.

returns

Returns are the unsold books that are returned from a bookseller to a publisher for credit. Hopefully your novel will not be among them. BILL

review copy [See also Reviews/Self-publishing]

A review copy is a free copy of your novel sent to a journalist, radio announcer et cetera (hopefully) for a positive review. PANDORA

reviews [See also Self-publishing/Sock-puppeting]

Reviews are comments about a novel that features in newspapers, magazines, radio, TV or online. Many reviewers review novels for a living. They enjoy and believe in promoting novels and the love of reading them to the public. A positive review indicating you have written a must-buy-novel is a great morale booster for an author. Good reviews are also extremely helpful for the marketing and sales of your novel. The blogging world has made reviewing more democratic and a useful online marketing tool. PANDORA

Ignore negative reviews. The reviewer was probably suffering from a night-on-the-town. Just keep writing.

rewrite

A rewrite is a writerly word meaning to edit your novel until it's as perfect as you can get it. The experience of most published writers is if you want to write well you must be prepared to rewrite. An editor can refer to a revision of a novel as a rewrite. If an editor suggests they're happy to review your novel if you're prepared to do a rewrite, do not submit your novel again unless you have reworked it and completed a rewrite. BILL

Another tack to take is to submit your novel to another agent or publisher as is. They may like it without the rewrite.

ritual [See also Procrastination/Routine]

A ritual is a series of fixed actions performed in a certain way. Many writers have rituals. For example: Earnest Hemmingway sharpened his pencils before he started writing. Rituals such as playing background music can help sharpen your focus. DIGBY

river [See also White space]

River aka a river of white is a publishing term to describe a coincidence of word spacing occurring in successive lines on a page forming an unwanted eye trap.

roman [See also Italic]

Roman is a publishing term for ordinary upright type—not italic.

romantic fiction [See also Frisson/URST/Vampire fiction]

Romantic, sometimes called relationship fiction, and now published under a prolific list of subgenres is a genre of novels about who-ends-up-with-whom or who-doesn't-end-up-with-whom. When you write romantic fiction you need to assure your reader you're telling the emotional truth about love. You have to convince your reader that in an ideal-world romantic love is possible. This can be difficult for a writer who's been dumped or is in the process of getting a divorce but it is doable. In romantic fiction you need a heroine with whom the reader can identify, and a hero the reader will want to marry, live with or have an affair with. If you're a half-glass-empty romantic-writer take comfort. The old familiar path for the happy-ever-after plot has vanished into cyberspace for heaps of romantic fiction subgenres. You can write a romance with elements of romance, underlying issues and messages. Or you can write a romantic-paranormal genre. In paranormal romances the vampire loves the heroine but he's also attracted to her blood. Your plot should show the path to love is never smooth but your heroine and hero, or heroine and heroine, or hero and hero, will win out in the end. GINA

For information about the multitude of subgenres within the main genre of romantic fiction, write to publishers, or trawl the Internet for publishers' websites.

rough [See also Graphic novel]

A rough is a publishing word for an artist's, or author's sketch, or a layout to be used as a guide for the graphic artist who is designing the cover and layout for your novel. LEE

routine [See also Ritual]

A routine is a usual or regular method of doing something. Develop a writing routine. Get used to sitting down at the same time every day. Sit down with a pen and paper, or at your computer, even if you don't have an idea in your mind. Don't wait for the muse or for inspiration—just write! VIOLET

Finish a writing session in the middle of a chapter, or leave a note so it's easy to pick up the next scene or chapter. This is better than staring at a blank screen or page when you start writing again.

royalties [See also Advance/Contract]

Royalties are a pre-agreed percentage of revenue the publisher will pay to you per copy of your novel (work) sold. Typically these will initially be set against your advance and when the advance has been earned out you will start receiving additional payments. BILL

If you are self-publishing you will not receive an advance, and you will have costs but you receive payment as you sell copies of your novel.

rules [See also Grammar]

Rules are the common order of things—a statement of what is allowed. If you're going to break a rule it's better to be aware of the rule you're breaking. There are a lot of so-called writing rules, more like conventions, such as how many points-of-view you should have in a scene, avoiding the use of passive voice, showing not telling, and watching your use of adverbs and adjectives. DAPHNE

It's a common belief there are only three rules for writing and fortunately no one knows what those rules are.

run [See also Self-publishing]

Run is the publishing term for the number of copies of a book to be printed. VIOLET

Don't go for big runs when self-publishing unless you have a large shed or garage for storage.

run-on [See also Self-publishing]

Run-on is a publishing term. It means to make sentences follow each other without a paragraph break. It can also mean to separate chapters by space rather than start each new chapter on a fresh page. VIOLET

run-on-passage writing [See also Sentence]

Run-on-passage writing is a long-sentence writing technique that can be used as practice for writers. The concept is to write for a three-minute time limit using one long sentence joined with words such as: and, then, so et cetera. After you've completed your long sentence shape it into shorter sentences. **DAPHNE**

Long sentences are usually 40-60 words. An average sentence length is 9-14 words. Remember today's readers have short attention spans.

running head/running foot [See also Folios/Self-publishing]

Running head and running foot are publishing terms for a title or brief descriptive heading printed as the header or footer of each page of your novel. **LEE**

If you're self-publishing and formatting an e-book, running heads and feet are deleted.

S

sacrifice

Sacrifice can mean to surrender something of value in order to gain something more valuable. If you want to write a novel you will have to sacrifice something you like doing in order to gain time to write your novel. Writing a novel is a long haul. It's hard work. What will you sacrifice? Make a list. Think about giving up that extra hour in bed in the morning, watching TV, or going to films et cetera. If you put time-spent-with-loved-ones on your sacrifice list you'll be a mean novel writer. However, you'd probably be a mean person no matter what you do. BIANCA

Keep a record of how many hours you spend watching TV and using social media. Then give up TV viewing, using social media and write your novel!

saddle stitching [See also Perfect binding]

Saddle stitching or saddle stapling are printing terms for a traditional bookbinding process. Pages are secured by a thread or wire staple drawn or punched through the spine fold. VIOLET

sale-or-return

Sale-or-return is a term that refers to a bookseller's right to automatically return unsold novels and receive credit from publishers. PANDORA

sans serif [See also Serif]

Sans serif is a typeface, such as Arial, and does not have short cross-lines at the end of the main straight vertical and horizontal strokes of letters. A sans serif typeface is usually reserved for use on smaller amounts of text that should be differentiated from the body copy (headings et cetera). VIOLET

SASE [See also Proposal/Online slush pile/Submitting your novel]

SASE (also called SSAE) is an abbreviation for a self-addressed stamped envelope. Send a SASE with a hard copy submission of your novel to an agent or publisher. This is for the return of your novel or for an editor or agent's reply. VIOLET

Very few publishers require hard copy submissions today.

satire

Satire is the use of words to show ridicule or exaggeration. Some novelists choose to write satirical novels. DIGBY

Watch you don't go OTT with satire. You can lose some readers.

scene [See also Mise en scene/Real-time scene]

A scene is a single event, action or series of connected actions taking place in a single setting in a finite period of time. Scenes can serve as structural blocks for your novel. Present scenes can echo previous scenes and foreshadow scenes to come. Strong scenes control turning points in your plot. Quiet scenes deepen character and work as transitional links between the strong scenes. Establish the rhythm of your novel by alternating strong active scenes with quiet, calmer scenes. A well-written scene can enrich characters, provide necessary information to the reader and move the plot forward. BILL

If you get stuck writing your novel start writing unconnected scenes to find your mojo again.

science fiction [See also Fantasy fiction/Speculative fiction]

Science fiction (commonly called sci-fi and often speculative fiction) is a genre that has all the elements of a novel, but the story is set in a scientific world. The fictional world inside your novel has to obey its own technological and scientific rules. These rules will dictate the characters you create, and the future-oriented action that drives your plot. Writing science fiction doesn't require a huge amount of technical knowledge. Hard sci-fi observes technical rigour, soft sci-fi is more interested in the social, cultural and philosophical aspects. Building your world is important. Science fiction can take place in the future or in an alternative version of Planet Earth as we know it. Think about where your characters live, what they do for a living, what they do for leisure and how they're governed et cetera. Conflicts can emerge from the world you have created, or specific characters. JOSH

Avoid info-dumping—giving long descriptions of settings or explanations of scientific or technological advances. It's important to give your reader key information but watch you don't hold up your story or your plot.

second-novel syndrome

The second-novel syndrome—also called the second-novel curse—is a fictional complaint for emerged authors. Writing the second novel has the reputation for being a huge obstacle. Most authors don't contract the second-novel syndrome. They find writing such grinding hard work they don't have time to worry about writing their second novel. It feels like it could be their third or eighth! VIOLET

> *Just deal with the page in front of you. Ignore your Greek chorus of doubt and doom.*

secondary research

[See also Historical fiction/Primary research/Research]

Secondary research is research based on writing by others, reasoning, or second-hand information. For example: information and facts found in periodicals, magazines, books, the Internet and films et cetera. DAPHNE

self-editing [See also Editing]

Self-editing is when a writer edits their own novel—draft after draft after draft. It's best to allow your final draft to cool down before a final self-edit. Read it aloud as a whole. Reading aloud forces you to read word by word. Edit for content and organisation. Then edit your novel to check it's pitched to your audience. Finally edit for language and style. Cut unnecessary individual words for example: *that, very, just and* of *the.* VIOLET

To make a major rewrite, copy and label the sections you want to rewrite. For example: description, setting, essential information, *and* necessary information *to feed in later. Paste these sections into a computer file, or paperclip hard copy pages together to work through, rewrite or delete. Keep the unused original sections to recycle later.*

selfies [See also Photographs]

Selfies are photographs authors can take of themselves using devices. Reviewed and selected with critical concern they could be useful to post on your blog, website or to use in marketing your novel. PANDORA

Members suggest you proceed with caution in the selection and use of Selfies for publicity.

self-publishing [See e-publishing path/Discoverability/POD]

Self-publishing is easy to do, but hard to do well. You can publish your novel, or outsource professional services to do a part (e.g. the cover, layout, editing or formatting) or you can undertake the complete process. If you've polished your manuscript to a professional level, and are happy to have your novel read and commented on, why not choose the self-publishing path? When you self-publish you need two different formats if you plan to issue your novel as print book and an e-book. Extensive technical knowledge is needed to format your novel for POD and e-book publishing. To self-publish both versions you need a faultless edit, a must-buy cover design and well-written panel copy. For a print version you need a 2-page design layout to compete with mainstream published novels on the market. E-books have a different internal formatting structure to print books. Digital-only provider companies convert a Word document to formats that fit e-book platforms along with the web-based companies like Kindle, Kobo and others that will appear on the horizon. Marketing, publicity and distribution channels are also vital to ensure the successful sale of your novel. LEE

> *The actual getting-your-novel-in-print or uploading your novel on-screen is relatively easy. The marketing and distribution to sell your novel is the hard part.*

semicolon (;) [See Emoticon/Colon/Punctuation]

A semicolon (;) is a punctuation mark. It was originally used to indicate to readers to take a longer pause than a comma, but a shorter pause than a colon. A semicolon is used to separate clauses or phrases that already have commas in them, or to separate parallel clauses where the joining word or conjunction (*and, but* et cetera) has been left out. For example: The dog looked for his bone in the bathroom; it wasn't there. The semicolon is useful for writers who like to write long but connected sentences. Sadly the semicolon seems to be on the wane. It was always an optional punctuation mark sharing a role with the comma and the full stop. Today it is often replaced with a full stop. JOSH

> *Ironically this subtle punctuation mark is surviving with the use of emoticons. For example ;-) meaning tongue-in-cheek.*

sentence [See also Object/Predicate/Subject]

A sentence is (usually) a group of words that has a subject, a verb and a predicate. A sentence begins with a capital letter and ends with a full stop, a question mark, an exclamation mark or an ellipsis (...). Sentences can be short or long depending on the writer's style. A sentence can even be just one word. For example: *Cool.* Too many long sentences using conjunctions such as *like, and, so, but,* et cetera can make tedious reading and slow your plot. You can break longer sentences with punctuation, dashes and brackets. BIANCA

Balance your writing with short and long sentences.

sentence fragments [See Fragment]

serendipity

Serendipity, meaning good things happening by chance, can play an amazing part in a writer's life. Serendipity comes from the fairy tale *The Three Princes of Sendip* in which the heroes possess the gift of making fortunate discoveries by accident.

Some writers find that once they are locked into their novel flashes of insight, lucky finds or meetings—almost like supernatural intervention—occur. For example, the exact reference book they're looking for can topple from a library shelf, the perfect solution for a plot issue pops up when they're watching a sitcom.

Some people classify moments of serendipity as a certain kind of good luck. Followers of Jung call it synchronicity. DAPHNE

serial comma [See also Comma]

The serial comma (also known as the Oxford comma) refers to the use of a comma between each item in a series of three or more words and it is always placed before the *and*—e.g. *red, white, and blue.* However some publishers and newspapers omit the final comma in a series e.g. *red, white and blue.* Either is correct. **DIGBY**

> *The key to sensible comma usage is a matter of good judgment. Ease of reading should be the main aim.*

series [See also Crime fiction/Fantasy fiction/Quels]

A series is a number of connecting novels and usually has the same characters, era, and setting. However, writers can stretch the definition. An author can divert from a contemporary setting and characters to explore the lives of the characters' ancestors. Sending the main character on a journey can provide new opportunities and conflicts for another book in the series. A writer can also allow a secondary character to take centre stage. Many crime fiction novels are written as a series using the one detective—or odd-couple-detecting-duo—one era and one place. Fantasy fiction and its many subgenres can develop into series. Writing a series of novels saves you a heap of research. **VIOLET**

> *If you've killed off your detective you can always write a pre-death novel for your series.*

serif [See also Sans serif]

A serif typeface (such as Times New Roman) has small short cross-lines at the end of the main straight vertical and horizontal strokes of letters. A serif typeface is usually preferred for body copy. **VIOLET**

setting [See also Description]

Setting is the background for your novel. Write about the

smells, the sounds, the tastes—as well as visual descriptions—to invoke a sense of place for your readers. A setting can often shape a novel. For example: the Arctic or a South American rainforest. Choosing an exotic setting for your novel can be a plus. However an exotic setting can mean expensive research if you feel you need to go there before you can write your novel. Places you know are easier to write about. BIANCA

If you set your novel in an unknown city e.g. New York you can use tourist guides, maps, directories, plus films, books and TV series as research tools. This cuts the expense of an actual visit.

shop-bought-cake lies [See also Don't talk about your novel!]

Shop-bought-cake lies are born when a friend asks about the incredible shop-bought cake you're serving with coffee. She says, *Did you make it?* And you reply with the lie, *Yes I did.* Then she asks, *Did you add lemon zest?* And... *How many eggs did you use?* And... *What did you add to the frosting?* Before you know it you find yourself telling one lie after the other. Beware of shop-bought-cake lies when friends inquire about your novel i.e. *Have you finished your novel?* Like it's been three years on the go. In a fit of pique you let a lie slip from your mouth. You answer, *Yes.* Then the next question follows. *Is it with an agent or publisher?* Next lie. *It's with a publisher.* And the next question? *Which publisher?* And so the shop-bought-cake lies, aka writing-a-novel lies continue. BIANCA

Avoid talking about your novel to non-writerly friends until you are published or your self-published novel is on the screen and/or in your hands.

show don't tell [See also Rules]

Show don't tell is a mantra especially relevant for beginning novelists. It means to dramatise rather than summarise the action in your novel—showing action rather than telling the reader equals more effective writing. For example: Violet left the Writers' Group meeting feeling very angry. The rewrite. 'I'm off!' Violet slammed the hall door when she left the meeting. **DAPHNE**

Members like the Chekov quote to explain Show don't tell. *Don't tell me the moon is shining, show me the glint of light on broken glass.*

side stitching

Side stitching, also known as side wiring, are old printing terms for a cheap method of securing sections of a book by inserting stiches (staples) through the first sheet to the last. **VIOLET**

signature [See also Perfect binding]

Signature in book binding refers to when pages are collected and folded into groups of four, eight or 16. Each group is called a signature.

simile [See also Figure of speech/Metaphor]

A simile makes a comparison using the words *like* or *as*. A simile should be as smooth as vanilla ice cream or like glace icing. Unusual similies are hard to find but they add magic to your text. **DAPHNE**

single-page summary [See also Elevator pitch/Logline/Synopsis]

A single-page summary is usually what an agent is looking for when they request a synopsis. A single-page summary should be about three to five paragraphs, and get into characters and their conflicts. It should explain the full story arc, including the ending of your novel. BILL

Don't think giving away the twist or ending in your single-page summary will ruin your plot. If something is irritating the agent or editor from reading your opening they will appreciate your novel more by knowing the ending.

slash

Slash (/), also called solidus, is a diagonal, forward-slanting stroke. It can be used to separate alternatives. For example: House/dog-sitter. The modern trend is to substitute the symbol with the word *slash*. For example: house-slash-dog-sitter. LEE

slush pile [See also Online slush pile/Submitting your novel]

The slush pile is a pile of unsolicited manuscripts waiting review in a publishing house. Some literary agencies also have a slush pile. The slush pile is usually stacked hard-copy submissions or online submissions waiting for a time when someone has the time and energy to attack the pile. In today's modern publishing scene, agents and publishers are finding books on e-published screen lists. VIOLET

smart reads [See also Marketing]

Smart reads are stories (350 words) sent out in episodes via smartphones to readers. The stories are crafted well with characters, dialogue and plot. Readers pay a small fee for each instalment they read on their smartphones. Smart reads can make excellent promotional material. PANDORA

smilies [See Emoticon]

SMS [See also Text messaging]

SMS, an abbreviation for short message service, relies on groups of acronyms strung together to make a form of mobile phone shorthand—common abbreviations. If you're writing a popular novel it's quite okay to use SMS in your novel. It could be the language of love between your characters in a romantic genre. Or a protagonist could use SMS as their language of choice to instruct an assassin to kill a character. The choices for using SMS in your novel are boundless. BIANCA

Members do not advise the use of SMS in your professional or deeply meaningful messages. It can lead to misunderstanding i.e. when you send SMS messages you're minus the facial and body language, which make messages so much more pleasing or sympathetic.

social media [See also Author platform/Platform/Social media following]

Social media is a common term to cover e-communication, which can be used by anyone, anytime and spreads everywhere via the Internet. There are various platforms such as email, Facebook, Twitter, Pinterest, YouTube, MySpace, blogs and websites. Social media can be an excellent source for authors in marketing and promoting their novels. PANDORA

Members advise novelists to think when writing posts, sending tweets or photos—whatever. Beware of the tempting, spontaneous factor of social media. Once you've pressed the send button information zaps into cyberspace And It Cannot Be Retrieved!

social media following [See also Author Platform/Online presence]

A social media following is to be desired for a writer. However, to acquire a following a writer needs a certain personality and a time budget that allows for a daily or even weekly commitment. Would your time be better spent in writing your novel? VIOLET

It's better not to venture into the world of social media if you feel it's not your cup of tea.

sock-puppeting [See also Reviews]

Sock-puppeting is a writerly word to refer to an unscrupulous novelist who anonymously writes up his or her own novel for online reviews and downgrades other novelists who write in similar genres. DIGBY

Avoid sock-puppeting at all times.

solicited manuscript [See also Proposal]

A solicited manuscript is a complete manuscript requested by the publisher or agent, usually in response to the query or proposal you've sent. BILL

space break [See also Dinkus]

A space break is a blank space (double, double space) on the page to indicate where one scene has ended and another begins. It's a standard practice to end one scene and lead-in for the opening of the next. BILL

spaghetti draft [See also Draft]

A spaghetti draft is a term used by some writers for their first draft, i.e. they throw everything at a wall and see what sticks. LEE

speculative fiction [See also Fantasy fiction/Horror fiction/Science fiction]

Speculative fiction is an umbrella term to cover the multitude of genres included in speculative fiction such as fantasy, science fiction and horror fiction et cetera. JOSH

Ignore comments such as 'Surely speculative fiction is a tautology?' Isn't all fiction speculative?

speech marks [See also Attributions/Dialogue/Quotation marks]

Speech marks or quotation marks are used to indicate when a character is speaking. Mainstream publishers have house style guides for usage. If you're a DIY publisher you can make your own choices about using speech marks—even ignore them completely. BIANCA

speech tag [See also Attributions/Direct Speech/Quotation marks]

Speech tag is a writerly term for an attribution. A speech tag shows how characters are sounding, or acting when they are speaking. *Said* is a very common speech tag to use when you are writing dialogue. BIANCA

spell check [See also Grammar check/Spelling styles/Typos]

A spell check, aka spelling checker, is a handy feature in a computer software package. In Microsoft Word a spell check feature is usually located under *Tools* and then *Spelling and*

Grammar. When you use it a wiggly red line will appear under the supposed incorrect spelling on your screen. The writer can then go to the spelling and grammar check to see alternates for their supposed incorrect spelling. A spell check will pick up errors but it will miss many. It will not locate a homonym, some typos, or a correct word in the wrong place. Turn your spell check off if you find it a distraction when you're writing your early drafts. Turn it on when you're editing. BIANCA

A dictionary is a great place to check spelling.

spelling [See also Spell check]

Spelling is putting letters in their correct order in words. A good writer uses correct spelling. Before submitting or uploading your novel correct all your typos, typing errors, and incorrect spelling. Use a dictionary as well as your computer spell check. BIANCA

If you're short on standard spelling skills get help before you submit your novel or self-publish.

spelling styles

Spelling styles differ. For example: British and American spelling styles. In many cases the British style has two spellings for one word, sometimes with different meanings for each word. For example: draught/draft. The American style has one spelling for both words for example: draft. Many countries vary between using the two styles such as Australia and Canada. DIGBY

You can adjust your dictionary and spell-check feature on your computer to specific languages, country of use and spelling styles.

spidergram [See Brainstorming/Mind mapping]

spine [See also Panel copy/POD]

The spine is the part of a book that joins the front and back cover. It is important to consider the design of the spine of a book if you're self-publishing. What will be written on it? You also have to consider that the spine copy will be read on an angle. Some countries have the spine text running right to left, other countries have the spine text running left to right. PANDORA

split infinitive [See also Grammar/Infinitive verb/Verb]

A split infinitive occurs when an infinitive verb such as *to dig* has another word between *to* and *dig*. An old grammar rule says, *Never split an infinitive!* For example: The dog likes to dig in Adrian's vegetable garden. This was considered correct. The dog likes *to frantically dig* in Adrian's vegetable garden. This was considered incorrect. Grammar purists like to avoid splitting infinitives at all costs, although it is no longer thought to be a high crime. If you do split an infinitive, watch you don't change the meaning of your sentence. DIGBY

spread

A spread is a design term for two pages. VIOLET

ST

ST is an abbreviation for a Single Title novel. BILL

stationery [See also Branding/Marketing]

Stationery such as writing paper with a personal letterhead, business cards, envelopes, labels and complement slips can project your brand and image. Think carefully about designing a logo—an identifying mark—and the selection of fonts, use of colour and quality of paper when you select personal stationery. These elements will contribute to your brand and give you standing as a professional writer. PANDORA

Some fonts such as Comic Sans attract hostility and choosing other fonts can indicate a lack of imagination for example: Times New Roman.

steamies [See also Young Adult novels]

Steamies refers to novels that fall into the mature Young Adult or New Adult category. The main ingredients in a Steamie is a good story that explores relationships and sexuality—the excitement and difficulties older teen-college-age characters discover in their journey to find out what they want in life. Steamies are realistic romances with engaging and exciting love stories. They are a quickly growing genre with a burgeoning market. DAPHNE

Sex in teen books is not new. Forever by Judy Blume was published in 1975.

steampunk [See also Science Fiction]

Steampunk is a subgenre of science fiction and fantasy novels heavily influenced by the steam power of the Victorian era. Some novels take place in present-day settings, in recognisable, historical periods or in fantasy worlds but they are based on the industrial revolution of the 19th century. The term *steampunk* was first coined in 1987 by the author K.W. Jeter to describe his and other Victorian fantasy novels. Over the last six to seven years the subgenre is becoming commonplace. DIGBY

Members advise writers to immerse themselves by reading novels in the subgenre if they want to write Steampunk novels. Remember: Imagination is everything!

story [See also Plot]

A story is the description of the chain of events in your novel i.e. your plot and subplots. BILL

To find your novel's story write for ten minutes using this start: This is a story about…

storyboard [See also Graphic novel/Structure]

A storyboard is usually notes and artwork in chart form or sequential boxes—like a comic book layout. An author can use a storyboard to plan the structure of their novel before the first draft. BIANCA

strapline [See also Elevator pitch/Logline/Premise]

The strapline is a snappy line on the cover of a novel. It's a marketing tool to catch the eye of the reader for a split second before they move on. PANDORA

structural editor [See also Editor/Mainstream publisher]

A structural editor, aka substantive, content or developmental, and commissioning editor in the world of publishing is the *big picture* editor. Structural editors read and access a manuscript for its structure. These editors edit the content, language and writing style of your novel. Their editing can include editing the story, characters, plot, theme, setting, et cetera. In the structural editing process an editor will suggest changes—even a major rewrite or restructure—so your novel has a cohesive shape, style and tone. They may suggest rewording and restructuring your novel to make it more accessible and clearer for the reader. The structural editing process is all about making your novel a great read. BILL

> *The title an editor has depends on the publisher they work for or according to the specific editing they do as an independent editor.*

structure [See also Epistolary fiction/Plot]

Structure refers to the framework—the scaffolding that holds your novel together. The structure you choose for your novel helps develop the plot. There are many structures to use when writing a novel such as:
* diary (written in a chronological series of events),
* time (using a day, a week, months of the year, season),
* time slip (writing in and out of the future or the past)
* letters or emails,
* a story within a story et cetera. BILL

stunt memoir

A stunt memoir is the latest genre of a fictional or non-fiction life story to hit bookshelves. Writers can dream up some project they are passionate about, blog and write about it in miniscule detail for about a year. For example: Giving up men—but just for a year, or writing about cooking every recipe in a famous cookbook. Hopefully your stunt memoir will be picked up and made into a film and/or best-selling novel. BIANCA

style [See also Commercial fiction/Literary novel /Voice]

Style, also called voice, is your writing that sets your novel apart from other writers. Style comes from what you are and who you are. Style is how a writer expresses themselves through their word choices and word order. A writer can change their style depending on the genre they're writing. For example: changing from a literary style when they write literary fiction, to a commercial style when they write crime fiction. VIOLET

Poor grammar, spelling and punctuation can hinder your style.

style sheet [See also Self-editing]

A style sheet, a word list, is a detailed publication-specific record used by editors and proofreaders to maintain consistency. It's used to keep up-to-date with editing decisions as a novel progresses. It is an alphabetical listing and can be divided into general style decisions. A style sheet is a running record of specific names, places, dates, punctuation marks, and words that have tricky spellings and may be represented in different ways. Making note of the preferred representation of a word, phrase, punctuation use, or a number helps you and the editor maintain consistency throughout your novel. GINA

A style sheet is also a great tool for writers—especially if you are self-publishing. Keep lists of names, places, spellings et cetera in alphabetical order as you write and rewrite your novel.

subject [See also Grammar/Object/ Predicate]

Subject is a grammatical term for the words in a sentence that represent the person, place, thing or idea that the sentence is about. For example: The little dog jumped over the dead pelican. *The little dog* is the subject. GINA

submitting your novel [See also Formatting/Pitch/Query]

Submitting your novel to an agent, mainstream or small indie publisher is a step to celebrate. Whether you write for therapy, a hobby, or to earn a living, it's perfectly acceptable to want to see your novel in print. Follow agents' or publishers' submission guidelines at all times when submitting your manuscript. Take note that many agents and publishers are only accepting electronic submissions. Don't submit your novel to an agent or publisher immediately upon completing it. Put your novel aside for a week or more. Edit it again. If publishers request hard copy submissions always use good quality white paper to print your novel, and number your pages in sequence. Correct formatting is essential. Your title page should show the book title, author's name, pen name if used, address, telephone and email address, and the approximate number of words in your novel. Enclose a short covering (query) letter introducing your novel, and your publishing record. Don't bind your manuscript. Use a stiff backing sheet and large elastic bands to secure your whole manuscript. Keep a clean hard copy of your novel in your files, and a clearly marked file on your computer. Keep track of your submissions—the date, name of agent and/or publisher. Be prepared to wait! Agents and publishers can take eight weeks or longer to decide if they wish to take you on as a client or publish your work. The above information is unnecessary if you are self-publishing. BILL

Don't be alarmed if your subconscious keeps on improving and editing your novel (even in your dreams) once you've submitted it. There is a subliminal dimension to the creative process.

subplot [See also Novella/Padding/Plot]

A subplot is a secondary plot running under the story of your novel. Multiple subplots create a complex novel. They are difficult to handle when you're doing a rewrite but they make for a great read. GINA

subsidiary rights [See also Contract/Electronic rights]

Subsidiary rights are additional opportunities for licensing your novel, above and beyond traditional book and e-book formats. Subsidiary rights are the various ways in which a novel may be reproduced, used or applied. These rights can include the right to print, publish and distribute the hardcopy or paperback editions for sale, foreign rights, audio book rights, film and television rights, the right to translate the novel and sell merchandise connected with your novel. The person or company who holds the ownership or license for these rights can direct how the work (your novel) can be used in each area. BILL

If you self-publish your novel you will need to negotiate these rights as they can be excellent sources of revenue. Professional societies and organisations for writers can assist you with questions re subsidiary rights.

suffix [See also Prefix/Word]

A suffix is a group of letters added to the end of a word or word-stem that add to or change the meaning of the word, for example: *pet+less = petless.* BIANCA

suspense [See also Crime fiction/Horror fiction]

Suspense in a novel is about giving your readers a sense of foreboding. Suspense needs to be carefully planned or thought out in order to produce shocks and reversals in the plot. Keep your readers wondering what will happen next. Suspense can grow out of characters. Move your characters around—give them actions and reactions. How your characters act and respond will drive the plot forward. Create sinister characters. Keep your reader guessing. Who are the bad guys? Will your protagonist throw her lot in with the bad guys? Short sentences and realistic dialogue are useful in creating suspense. LEE

If you use first person viewpoint and the story is told by the narrator I, and if the narrator dies, someone else—maybe his ghost or spirit can continue to tell the story.

suspension of disbelief [See also Imagination]

Suspension of disbelief is a phrase attributed to the famous writer Coleridge. If you're writing a novel and you want your readers to believe what you're writing, you want your readers to suspend disbelief. For example: if you're writing a novel where your main character lives underwater, you want your readers to believe she can *really* live underwater. You want to transport your readers to a watery world—suspend their disbelief. BIANCA

symbols

Symbols written into a novel give commonplace objects a symbolic possibility. They can make the abstract concrete for your reader. For example: a bird in flight can symbolise freedom, an egg—fertility, a snake—evil. Dreams are made of symbols. Use the symbols your subconscious mind creates and weave them into your novel. For example: a dream about a huge black rat can be a symbol for a ratfink partner you are creating in your romantic novel. GINA

synonym [See also Antonym/Thesaurus]

A synonym is a word with a similar meaning to another. For example: huge/big, great/massive. A thesaurus is a useful tool if you're looking for synonyms. DIGBY

synopsis [See also Book description/Blurb/Single-page summary]

A synopsis is a selling tool for your novel. A synopsis is a summary of the highlights of your novel (with the ending) submitted to an agent or publisher as part of a proposal. Many agents or publishers will be looking for a synopsis no longer than one, two or three pages.

Other agents or publishers may request a longer synopsis. Check agents' and publishers' guidelines for the format they require. A synopsis is traditionally written in third person and in the present tense. Present events in the same order they occur in the novel. Begin with a plot-conflict hook, and your protagonist's motivations and emotions. Stay invisible as the writer. Writing techniques should be smoothly interwoven into your synopsis. If you're self-publishing you will need a book description and back copy. These take the place of a synopsis but you don't give away the ending. BILL

Your synopsis can be your foot-in-the-door to reach an agent or publisher. Master the art of synopsis writing. Polish your synopsis until it's perfect.

syntax [See also Grammar]

Syntax is a word to describe the grammatical rules of a language and the way in which words are arranged to form phrases and sentences. DIGBY

a system backup [See also Backup options/Cloud/USB flash drive]

A system backup for your digital files requires special software that can be purchased and installed on your computer. A system backup such as those used by businesses can restore your files after computer failure to the point where you last did your backup. BILL

T

talks [See also Branding/Marketing/Marketing tools]

Talks are frequently overlooked as excellent marketing tools to sell your novel. You can either talk about your life as a writer, your writing process, a completed novel or your work in progress. You can read segments from your novel relating to characters, setting or your plot. You can give talks at local libraries, community centres, literary luncheons, writers' circles, bookshop events et cetera. You'll probably have to offer your speaking services for free if you do a library talk, but this can be a win-win situation if more borrowers borrow your novel and you are registered for Library Lending Rights. You may be paid a fee if you're teaching some aspect of writing or you're the after-dinner speaker at a high-end event. If you're rising to celeb-author status you can join a speakers' agency and they will organise gigs for you. Choose and mark passages from your book to read—more than you need. Time and/or tape yourself reading the said passages. Practise reading with (and without) a podium to rest your novel. Allow and be prepared for a Q & A session at the end of your talk or reading. VIOLET

> *It's a good idea to have a friend in the audience who can ask one or two questions in case there is a patch of deadly silence after your talk. Always take copies of your novel with you to sell and sign or arrange for a local bookseller to be at your talk.*

tautology

Tautology is writing or saying the same thing twice. For example: *a bare bone*. The absolute truth. DIGBY

technique [See also Literary devices/Writing classes and workshops]

Technique in the writerly world refers to the nuts and bolts—also called literary devices—a writer needs to write their novel. A writer rarely needs encouragement to write but they may need help with the technical aspects of using language such as grammar, punctuation, metaphors, similes et cetera. Make a list of writing techniques you're unsure of. Avoid using them until you know how to use them. Start with the top of your list e.g. similes. Teach yourself how to write similes. BIANCA

There are a vast number of how-to books written about grammar. Check them thoroughly. Ninety per cent of books will be useless, ten per cent useful. The ten per cent of books you find useful will be a different ten per cent another novelist will find useful.

techno know-how [See also Backup]

Techno know-how is important for a writer. Keeping up-to-date with technology can assist you in writing your novel. For example: knowing the best and latest ways to back up your novel and using social media for networking. You also need to be aware of your characters' techno know-how and technical backgrounds. Be aware of the technology available in the time you've set your novel. If you're writing crime fiction in a Victorian setting, forensic science processes won't be available to check invisible bloodstains in the horse-carriage. Do you need to bring digital aspects of your novel into the 21st century?

For example: Do your characters blog, communicate by email, text, post on Facebook, YouTube or tweet et cetera? Could your protagonist be dumped by email? Will your antagonist plan a murder using Google in her home office or plan the murder on the public library computer? JOSH

Another example: Will your protagonist Google, instead of using a telephone directory or copy of Who's Who to locate info vital to your plot?

technology

Technology has come between the hand and the written word. Digital word-processing features such as cut, paste, copy, delete, footers and headers, page numbering, word counts, inserting date and time of writing, highlighting as well as Googling when you need to verify a fact are here to stay. They have their benefits for time-short writers. VIOLET

tense [See also Grammar/Verb]

The tense of a verb tells when an action takes place. There are three main tenses—present, past and future tense. For example: I am Googling. (Present tense) I have Googled. (Past tense) I will Google. (Future tense) DIGBY

Watch your use of tenses in your novel. Be consistent.

territory [See also Contract/Publishing right]

Territory is related to selling rights for a novel in a territory or country. This means you could sell English rights to a company in the US for publication in North America while also selling English rights to a company in the UK for publication in the UK and Commonwealth. Your agent or publisher will negotiate these rights to sell your novel. If you're self-publishing you will do the negotiating. BILL

National societies of authors and literary lawyers have advisory services for writers to assist in negotiating contracts and rights for their novels.

tetralogy [See also Series]

A tetralogy is a term for four related novels. LEE

text messaging

Text messaging is sending and receiving a message on a device. The informal abbreviated messages exploit many traditional features of spelling in English. Letters and numbers are used for syllables or words. For example: *b there at 4, c side, fish n chips, C u 2morrow, gr8, l8er, w8ng. r u up 4 it, 4tun8, 4evr.* Letters are omitted. For example: *fxd (fixed), txtin (texting), spk (speak).* Eye-dialect (unusual sounds with odd spellings) is used. For example: *wot, nite, rite, fite, iz, kool.* And pop spelling is used. For example: *beva, aft, ya, dis, der, dey.* Et cetera. JOSH

Some members accept using cuz for because but think it's just as quick to write was than wuz.

that/which [See also Pronouns]

That and Which are relative pronouns and can be confusing words for writers. They are used to begin clauses that describe a noun or pronoun. Both words are used if the noun is a place, animal, or thing. *That* is used for meaning. For example: The dog *that* lives with Gina is cute. *Which* is used for a clause that isn't essential to the meaning, and is enclosed by a comma. For example: Bill Kruger has written the novel, *which* is for sale in Pages gallery. Some writers overdo the use of *that*. When you see or write the word *that*, try reading the sentence without *that*. If the sentence makes sense without *that*, delete *that*. GINA

There are frequent arguments over the use of that *or* which *between members. In modern usage it's common to use* that *or* which *equally.*

the [See also 'a' and 'an']

The is an essential and simple word known in grammatical terms as a definite article. *A* and *an* are known as indefinite articles. *The* can be used in front of all nouns, singular or plural. For example: I bought the bestseller on Saturday, and by the end of *the* week I'd read *the* novel. DIGBY

their/there/they're

Their, There and They're are frequently used incorrectly by writers. The use of *their* shows possession of an object. For example: That is *their* van. *There* refers to a physical or abstract place. For example: I'm going over *there* to write. *There* is a wonderful bookstore in Shelly Beach. *They're* is a contraction of *they are.* For example: *They're* finally writing. DIGBY

theme

A theme is the global view of your novel, the message underlining it. For example: the seven deadly sins—lust, gluttony, greed, sloth, wrath, pride and envy make great themes for a novel. Knowing your novel's unifying theme makes it a lot easier to write. GINA

You may not have a theme before you write your novel but you probably will when you finish writing your novel.

thesaurus [See also Antonym/Synonym/Tools of the trade]

A thesaurus is reference book about words. It is organised alphabetically in order for the user to find synonyms and antonyms. *Roget's Thesaurus* is a famous and fascinating collection of words of closely related meanings. A thesaurus is an excellent tool for an author searching for the right word to write. Most computer software packages include a Thesaurus feature. JOSH

a third of the way through...
[See also Novella/30,000-word questions]

A third of the way through... your first draft—about 30,000 words—can be a very difficult time for writers. You've been writing a long time and you still have a long way to go. You feel like giving up. The trick is to refuse to give up. Just write another 10,000 words. This will get you to 40% of your novel—halfway there if you're writing an 80,000-word novel. Writing the second half is all downhill. BILL

Skip to scenes you've thought of and write them. You can fill the gaps and tidy up all the ends when you get to the end of your first draft.

30,000-word questions [See also Word count]

30,000-word questions are questions writers ask when they've written about 30,000 words of their novel. They are: Q1 - *Why am I doing this?* and Q2 - *How can I get to the end?* The answer to Q1 should be: *You're writing a novel because you want to.* And the answer to Q2 is: *You can get to the end if you write 1000 words a day for 50 days.* GINA

Find time. Get up early or stay up late. Give up TV, movies, trawling on the Internet and wasting time on social media. Get the first draft of your novel down and over the line. Polish it later.

the 3-drafts writing process [See also Draft]

The 3-drafts Writing Process is an effective way to produce a reasonable novel.

* **Draft One** is when you go for it and simply keep count of the words or pages. Relax and have fun.

* **Draft Two** is when you analyse what you have written. Check out the connection between scenes and chapters. Rewrite. Cut and paste—in real life or use word processing features—the best parts you have written. Word of caution: keep a file of everything you cut.

* **Draft Three** is when you work as hard as you can to make your novel the best it can be. BILL

Eventually you will have to walk away and pass your novel into other hands.

thriller [See also Crime fiction/Whodunits]

A thriller is a subgenre of crime fiction novels. A thriller can be a mix of genres such as neo-gothic, detective procedural, forensic, psychological crime fiction. A best-selling thriller usually has a complex layered plot and characters that live in a believable world. If you have experience as a task force detective, undercover cop, neuroscientist, or psychiatrist this experience is a great asset in writing a thriller. Otherwise the answer is to research in order to write plausible dialogue and a plausible plot. LEE

Best-selling authors of thrillers are reputed to earn millions of dollars in royalties from their novels. They usually manage to write a thriller a year in time for the Christmas and holiday markets.

a ticking bomb

A ticking bomb is a writerly phrase to describe a time line that is pushing the story forward and keeps the reader turning the pages of your novel. The ticking bomb can be something that is foreshadowed and will cause change or it can be an overall feeling from the way you write the novel. DAPHNE

timeline [See Plotline]

time-slip novel [See also Historical fiction/Research]

A time-slip novel has parallel storylines. It covers two different periods of time. Both periods of time are written for the reader as if they are in real time. Neither the past, nor the present stories are written as flashbacks.

The historical elements in a time-slip novel may require research so your readers will know what your characters look like, what they'll be wearing, the transport they're using, the settings they'll be living in et cetera. A timeline of dates, times and places where events take place is useful to organise the time-slip structure of your novel and keep track of your plot. This can be included as a chronology in the back pages of your novel. DAPHNE

> *Distinct chapter headings or divisions in your novel can help the reader to quickly adjust to different times.*

title [See also Cover]

A title is the first selling point—a signpost—for readers scanning a shelf of novels, a list of titles or thumbprint-size covers online. The three, four or eight words on a cover can make all the difference to your novel being read or passed over. Single word titles are great—easy for readers and book buyers to remember. Titles have no copyright. You are legally entitled to use a title already used by another author. Don't be precious about your title. Authors can be too close to their work to judge how it might be best summed up in a catchy, commercial title that will sell thousands of copies. And don't spend hours trying to think of a title. Use a working-title while you are writing your novel. When a publisher accepts your novel they will probably change the title. Publishers have title-know-how when it comes to knowing what titles are trendy and marketable. Check the web so duplication of your title is avoided. If you're self-publishing choosing your title is your decision. VIOLET

Titles should indicate what your novel is about e.g. The Compost-bin Murder. You always knew what Agatha Christie's novels were about, e.g. Murder on the Orient Express.

TK

TK is an old writerly symbol meaning *to come*. Use this symbol as you write your novel when you're unsure of a fact or need to add details or descriptions later. VIOLET

to/too/two

To/Too/Two are three simple words that are confusing and frequently escape the spell check. To is a preposition that begins a prepositional phrase. For example: We went *to* the writers' festival. (Preposition.) *To* is also used with a verb to form an infinitive. We live *to* read novels. (Infinitive). *Too* is an adverb that means excessively or also. *Two* is the number. DAPHNE

too many red herrings

[See also Red Herring/Crime Fiction/Chekov's Rifle]

Too many red herrings is a phrase that refers to cluttering your crime novel with too many objects or snips of detail. Cluttering your novel with irrelevant details confuses the reader. Nothing in your novel should be random—except calculated red herrings. Dispose of any unnecessary objects or details that don't move your story forward. VIOLET

tools of the trade [See also Dictionary/Laptop/Thesaurus]

Tools of the trade—pen and paper—are a writer's basic needs. One famous writer uses a pencil she sharpens with her deceased father's penknife. This is cool. Few writers would still be using *P and Q*—parchment and quill—although many early novels were written with these tools i.e. Jane Austen. (Maybe not Jane Austen. She probably used a pen and kept dipping it in an inkwell. Moving on.) If you hand-write or use a typewriter to write your novel, you'll need to transfer your novel to a computer file if you want it to be read by an agent, publisher, or published online. Many writers begin their novel, or write parts of their novel, using a pen and notebook. Then they work on a computer. Computers are excellent tools for writers. If you key quickly you can keep up with the whizzy stuff in your head. Computers come after the invention of the wheel and cuneiform script on the *Writers' Top 10 Inventions List*. Reference books such as a dictionary, thesaurus, and a good book on grammar and punctuation are also absolutely vital tools for writers. Depending on your budget you can keep adding to your writer's bookshelf with writerly references or use Google to access these tools. BIANCA

Computer word-processing packages have features such as spell and grammar checks and a thesaurus. These features are great tools for writers. If you're unaware of these features stop, take time out to become familiar with them.

tone [See also Style/Voice]

The tone of a novel can be formal or informal and is connected with the style of the writer. Tone is when a writer controls their novel through their choice of words and sentences. BILL

track changes [See also Editing/Self–editing]

Track Changes is a commonly used feature in Microsoft Word software. *Track Changes* allows you to edit your novel by making deletions or additions. Clicking Review on the menu, then Track Changes, can activate this feature. When you use *Track Changes* it allows writers and editors to edit and comment on writing across distances with speed and ease. Inserted text shows up in colour, deleted text is shown with *strikethrough*. Additions appear in a different colour and underlined—a different colour for each person making or accepting the edits. Deletions and comments are shown in annotation balloons alongside the text. You can see who made the edits, add comments and click to choose or reject an edit. Many editors use *Track Changes* when they work with writers in editing their novel through the different steps. BILL

Track Changes is useful when writers share their writing with colleagues for editing and feedback online.

traditional publishing [See Mainstream publishing]

traditional publishing process
[See Mainstream publishing process]

trademark symbol (™)

The trademark symbol (™) is used to denote that you have permission to write about a product in your novel. Some novels are written as a platform to specifically promote products for a company. It's assumed the author would have done a deal with a big brand name company. PANDORA

transitions [See also Drop down/Flashback]

Transitions are words, phrases or other writerly techniques to move your writing from one scene to another. *For example: When... The next day... et cetera.* Transitions occur most often between scenes and chapters. As a novelist it's your job to steer your reader through your novel scene by scene, chapter by chapter. Every scene must evolve logically from the previous scene in order to provide continuity of plot. Use a variety of transitions. Using different typefaces, or formatting within your novel, can make a transition to the next event. (Some editors don't approve of this.) Diary entries, journals, letters and quotes can become transitions and set up a new scene. Flashbacks (in or out of italics) can also work as transitions. Make sure you transition smoothly in and out of a flashback. BILL

translation right [See also Contract/Publishing Right]

Translation right is the right you sell the right to a publisher to translate your novel into another language and sell the foreign-language edition of the book in the territories where that language is spoken. Your agent or publisher will negotiate selling these rights—if you're self-publishing you'll need to do the negotiating. PANDORA

transport the reader [See also Imagination]

Transport the reader is a writerly term. As a writer your job is to transport—figuratively speaking—your reader to an imagined reality. You only have the marks you make on white surfaces or on a screen to do this. DIGBY

trim size [See also Perfect binding]

Trim size is the final size of a print book—width and height—after it has been trimmed. VIOLET

trope [See also Cliché]

A trope is a significant or recurrent theme or motif. A trope can add to a character or plot and move the story on. However a trope can be overused and become a cliché. *For example: a grumpy old man.* VIOLET

> *You don't want to create characters and situations readers identify with too easily.*

Trojan [See also Backup]

A *Trojan* is online software that can take control of PCs. It can sneak into your computer and attack it while it pretends to be something else. It could replace your novel file with a different version. Use protection software if you're writing your novel using a computer. JOSH

TV and dramatisation rights [See also Contract/Publishing right]

TV and dramatisation rights cover companies who want to

dramatise your novel for television or radio plays. Your agent or publisher can negotiate to sell these rights for you. If you're self-publishing you do your own negotiating. BILL

> *Always have a logline for your novel on hand re a query to dramatise your novel for TV.*

Twitter [See also Social media/Viral marketing]

Twitter is a huge social media site for short forms of e-communication. Twitter can be a useful social media to promote your latest novel. It's another place where you can be followed by prospective readers and where you can publicise your novel. You can *twitter, twit,* or *tweet* using 140-characters to create miniature—frequently amusing—writing gems. It's an excellent viral marketing tool to help sell your novel. However it can become annoying for receivers of your tweets if you tweet too often. And it could cause issues if you tweet indiscriminate tweets. PANDORA

> *Twitter will not advance your writerly reputation if you constantly tweet rubbish.*

typeface [See also Font/Sans Serif/Serif]

Typeface refers to the type design or font such as Times New Roman selected for the body of text for your novel. Fonts like Times New Roman with cross-strokes (serifs) and varying line-widths are considered better for continuous text used in books. Fonts like Gill Sans and Verdana without cross-strokes (sans serifs) and with even width are better for short display pieces of text. Most publishers require writers to submit novels in Times New Roman or in Times fonts. JOSH

> *What you know as a font is a digital version of a typeface.*

typesetting [See also POD (Print on Demand)/Proofreading]

Typesetting is placing the text on pages as it will appear when your novel is printed as a hard-copy book. This is the stage when page numbers are added. If you're taking the DIY publishing path and the POD (Print on Demand) process you will need to take particular care at the typesetting stage of the process. LEE

typewriter [See also Computer/Laptop/Qwerty keyboard]

The typewriter, formerly spelt Type Writer, was the first technical device that speeded the writing process for writers. In 1876 Sam Clemens (Mark Twain) became the first author to produce a book-length manuscript *The Adventures of Tom Sawyer*, aided by the Type Writer. Over time Type Writer became one word—typewriter. Typewriters became portable, electric, some electric and portable. The keys operated on a piano principle, along with the sliding carriage, were superseded in some machines by the spinning, shifting ball element. Today computers still use the typewriter's QWERTY keyboard. Some writers like to use an old typewriter when they come to a hard place in their novel. Pounding on typewriter keys helps sort out their writing. However most writers won't miss the retyping, erasing, real-time cutting and pasting that went with writing a novel on a typewriter in the past. DIGBY

To re-ink a used typewriter ribbon use a few drops of sewing machine oil. Pull the ribbon tight and let it sit for a week. Some writers use a typewriter—presumably portable—placed on their knees to write their novel. This is not recommended.

typo [See also Spell check]

A typo is a spelling or a punctuation mistake made through

typing the wrong keys. Typos frequently pass through a computer spell check because they are legitimate words but used in the wrong context. For example: weak or week, sweet or tweet, My goat (goal) is to complete my novel by Christmas. **DAPHNE**

> *A typo in publishing terms is called a* literal—*the omission of letters in words by the typesetter. Watch out for them when you receive proofs of your novel.*

typographical conventions
[See also Self-publishing/Submitting your novel]

Typographical conventions such as exclamation marks, italics, all caps, and bold should be used *infrequently*, RARELY!!! when you submit your manuscript to an agent or publisher or self-publish. **VIOLET**

U

unjustified type [See also Justified type]

Unjustified, or ragged type, is type that is set flush against the left-hand margin, the right, or neither. VIOLET

upload [See also e-book/e-publishing path/DIY publishing]

Upload is an e-publishing term that refers to pressing a key to upload—to send your novel into cyberspace to be e-published and/or to sell online. JOSH

You need to prepare well before you upload.

unplug the Internet

Unplug the Internet while you write your novel is good advice. The Internet is an invaluable tool for writers but at times it can be more like an enemy than a friend. Do not check your email or check *that* blog while you are writing your novel. Before you know it you will have wasted an hour or two and you will not have added one sentence to your potentially best-selling novel. DAPHNE

Some writers retreat and use old technology—vintage typewriters and pen and paper—to avoid the distraction of the Internet. Other writers use a second computer in another room—a computer that is not connected to the Internet—to write their bestsellers. There are apps you can install on your computer to lock you out of the Internet when you are writing the novel.

unsolicited manuscript [See also Query/Submitting your novel]

An unsolicited manuscript is a manuscript sent to a publisher—a manuscript they did not specifically ask to see. BILL

upper case lettering [See also Alphabet/Lower case lettering]

Upper case lettering is a term used in word processing and typesetting software for capital letters. The term originated in the early days of printing. Sets of alphabetical ordered letters were kept in large wooden cases placed on sloping racks. The larger sized letters were kept in the upper section of the cases because printers used them less often than the smaller letters. Smaller letters were kept handy in the lower cases. VIOLET

If you use upper case letters, capitals, in emails it indicates you're very annoyed.

URST [See also Frisson/Romantic fiction]

URST is the abbreviation for the writerly term, *unresolved sexual tension,* used by romantic novel writers, screen and playwrights. URST keeps your readers turning the pages of your novel. In some romantic fiction genres, it's important to write about the emotions of desire rather than the actual sexual act. The writer needs to keep percolating the intoxicating dream of love on the pages of their romantic novels. BIANCA

USB

USB, aka flash drive, is a small portable device. It is easy to use to copy digital files. They are affordable for writers on limited budgets and can hold large amounts of data according to their individual capacity. JOSH

Members recommend writers use USB flash drives to back up their novels—keep one USB at home, one in the garden shed or garage, and one in a wallet or handbag. If you're going to carry your files with you consider putting your USB flash drive on a key ring or lanyard to reduce the risk of losing it.

using an existing character [See also Characters]

Using an existing character from a novel written years ago to write the character in your novel, depends on the date the original author and creator of the character dropped off the twig. For example: James Benmore wrote *Dodger (Querus)*, which continues the story of Jack Dawkins, the artful dodger in *Oliver Twist* written by Charles Dickens, Charles Dickens having died 175 years ago. Copyright in the UK, USA and Australia lasts for 70 years from the end of the year in which the author died. If the novel was written longer than 70 years ago—you can proceed to write a novel around an existing character. If the original author was deceased more recently you may need permission from the author's estate. Some famous authors have been requested by authors' estates to write sequels. For example Susan Hill was requested by the Daphne Du Maurier Estate to write a sequel to *Rebecca*. VIOLET

Many authors have written successful novels and enjoyed continuing the journey of characters created by a deceased author but beware of dedicated fans of the original novels. Most fans will not be happy.

V

vampire fiction [See also Genre/Zombie fiction]

Vampire fiction has been a popular genre producing bestsellers in the paranormal romantic and Young Adult subgenres. However the appeal of vampires seems to be fading. Stories of vampires date back to ancient Babylonia and public fascination with vampires began in the Middle Ages. Bram Stoker's 1897 novel *Dracula* was a gruesome but popular tale. In recent times vampires have developed into tragic, poetic, brooding characters. Stephanie Meyer's *Twilight series* and Anne Rice's *Vampire Chronicle novels* have become bestselling series. **DAPHNE**

It's fruitless to try and guess the next hot genre. Just write what you want to write.

vanity publishers [See also DIY publishing/Self-publishing]

Vanity publishers are publishing companies that charge an author the costs of printing his or her novel. They usually accept a book regardless of the quality. The intended market is the author rather than readers. Marketing tends to be minimal or non-existent. **VIOLET**

verb [See also Adverb/Grammar/Participle]

A verb is a word that tells what the subject of a sentence is doing, behaving or feeling. No sentence is complete without a verb. A lone verb can even make a complete sentence. For example: Dig! Go for strong verbs. They create great word pictures. A verb agrees with its subject in person and number. For example: I (or you, we or they) live in Shelly Beach. The tense of a verb tells us when an action takes place. For example: I am Facebooking. I have Facebooked. I will Facebook. **DIGBY**

If you feel you need to know more about verbs and their uses, bone up on authoritative grammar texts.

verso [See Numbering pages]

viewpoint [See POV]

vice versa

Vice versa means the other way round. It comes from Latin, meaning reversed. **DIGBY**

video book trailers [See also Book trailer/Social media]

Video book trailers are effective tools for promoting your book. The style and content of them is limitless. A hybrid trailer is a combination of a F2F meeting with an author and the synopsis of the book. Video book trailers can be an efficient non-text press release to grab the attention of your target audience—agents, editors, readers and librarians. Video book trailers can be fun ways to promote and attract young readers if you are writing middle grade or young adult novels.

You as the author can engage in an interview with a cartoon representation of your characters. JOSH

Be strategic with the distribution of your video book trailer.

viral marketing [See also Branding/Marketing/Self-publishing]

Viral marketing—aka viral advertising—are buzz words used for marketing techniques on social media networks such as Facebook, Twitter, YouTube, blogs and websites or spreading advertising from person to person. Viral marketing is an excellent way to publicise and sell your novel. PANDORA

Beware: Viral marketing can turn around and bite you.

virus [See also Backup]

A virus is a disruptive software program spread by computer users who unwittingly trigger it after clicking on an infected online file. LEE

Install protective software on your computer to protect your work-in-progress.

vocabulary [See also Word/Word-of-the-week Event]

Vocabulary is the list of words writers know and use. The English language has over 600,000 words. Shakespeare used 20,000 words when he was writing his plays. Writers can increase their vocabulary by using reference books such as dictionaries, thesauruses and learning a word-a-day. New words are constantly being introduced into the English language. For example: Facebook, Google, and blog are now used as nouns and verbs. BIANCA

voice [See also Active voice/Passive voice/Style]

Voice is a writerly word used for a writer's style. Active voice and Passive voice are grammatical terms. DIGBY

vowels [See also Word/Language/Sentences]

Vowels—*a, e, i, o, u*—are five letters in the English alphabet. The other twenty-one letters—*b, c, d, f, g, h, j, k, l, m, n, p, q, r, s, t, v, w, x, y, z*—are called consonants. VIOLET

W

web presence [See Author platform/Platform]

webinar [See also Blog tour/Writers' conferences]

A webinar is a conference, seminar or interactive workshop that is held online via the Internet. Participants can share and interact in real-time and across locations. Webinars are useful events for writers to share and connect with each other. BILL

website [See also Social media/Viral marketing]

A website is an excellent marketing tool for a novelist. It's a shop window for your books. You can list details of books you've written and put links to bookshops and online sites where your books are available.

You can design your own website, or pay a web designer to design one for you. Websites are also valuable to use for research. Use appropriate key words to locate authentic and specific websites for your research. BILL

Beware you don't get tangled in a web of websites instead of writing your novel.

what if? [See also Serendipity]

What if? is a key question fiction writers can ask about their characters, plot—whatever. Asking the question *What if?* can provide random solutions if you come to a bump in your writing. It also helps if you accept that intuition, synchronicity or serendipity can inspire and assist you in sorting problems in your novel. DAPHNE

what's at stake? [See also Plot/Protagonist]

What's at stake? is a vital question to ask about your protagonist. A strong plot always has something at stake for the protagonist—a life-and-death issue for your main character. Is there enough at stake for the main character in your plot? This conflict should define the first act of your plot. LEE

where can I send my novel?

[See also Finding a publisher/DIY publishing/ Genre]

Where can I send my novel? is a question writers ask when they complete their novels The easy answer is to send a literary novel to publishers who publish literary novels, a commercial novel to publishers who publish commercial novels.

If you're writing a specific genre or a subgenre of a genre, find a publisher that specialises in publishing your specific genre, subgenre or sub-subgenre. BILL

Check out bookshops, libraries and websites to see what publishers are publishing.

which/witch [See also That/Which and Who/Which]

Which and Witch are confusing words for some writers. Which is a relative pronoun used to begin a clause to describe a noun or pronoun. Witch is a noun for a fantasy character. For example: Which witch is out to get you? DIGBY

If you use these two words incorrectly they will not be picked up by your spell check.

white space [See also Self-publishing]

White or empty space is a term used in designing page layouts. White space provides a rest for readers' eyes. Publishers design novels using white space based on decades of experience to make novels attractive and easy to read. Allowing for white space is important if you're self-publishing. The use of space as a layout tool can affect the cost of printed publications. VIOLET

who/whom [See also Pronouns/Whose/Who's]

Who and Whom are problem pronouns that can confuse writers.
* **Who** is the subjective form, acting as the subject form of a noun. For example: *Who* [subject] will close the hall?
* **Whom** is the objective form acting as the object of a verb. For example: Whom [object) did they say wrote the novel? DIGBY

In modern writing whom is rarely used.

whodunits [See also Crime fiction/Red herring]

Whodunits, also called *cosies*, are a genre of traditional mystery fiction—fiction that contains a puzzle to be solved. The sleuth protagonist must find the *who*—in Whodunit. Traditional whodunits are set in a closed setting. For example: a country manor house, a cruise ship, a hotel, a seaside town. About ten characters are developed as suspects. The plot should get thicker and thicker as you introduce more clues, red herrings and suspects. The plot should unravel without the assistance of forensic or psychological profiles. The reader should be guessing what happened until about the last chapter—or page.

A basic whodunit structure has the usual structure for a novel of a beginning, a middle, and an end. In the beginning the victim, the person who finds the body, the scene of the crime and the detective—sleuth, detective or private eye—are introduced. The middle is when the suspects are interviewed or investigated by the sleuth. The end is where the suspects are eliminated and the writer can zero in on the crime and the perpetrator. All clues and red herrings must be explained by the end of the novel. VIOLET

If you don't want another writer to resurrect your detective or sleuth character—kill him off. Agatha Christie killed off her detective, Hercule Poirot so others couldn't screw up her character. However you can bring your detective back to life. Set your novel in a time before he or she was killed.

whose/who's

Whose and Who's are two words that can confuse writers.

* **Whose** is the possessive form of who. For example: Whose manuscript was left in the Community hall?
* **Who's** is the contracted form of *who* and *is*. For example: Who's [who is] taking the writing tasks to photocopy for the next meeting? DIGBY

widow [See also Orphan]

A *widow* is a typographic term for a short last line of a paragraph or a line consisting of only a single word at the top or bottom of a page. Widows look odd on a page and should be avoided. VIOLET

Watch out for orphans and widows when you self-publish. They are considered errors in print design, look unattractive and should be eliminated.

WIP [See Work-in- progress]

word [See also Vocabulary/Word-of-the-week]

A word is the smallest collection of letters used for meaning. Words are amazing. They can be weapons and tools—hopefully used for good! When writers choose words for their novels they create another world for readers. Words come and go. New words are always being invented e.g. blogosphere. Always check a dictionary or thesaurus if you're unsure of a word. Ask yourself—do I know this word? If you don't, don't use it. Use a word you do know. Keep reading to enlarge your vocabulary. DIGBY

Keep your dictionary at your side, or a dictionary accessible on the screen at all times.

word count

A word count can keep your mind focused on your goal of completing your novel. The word-count feature on a word-processing package is an invaluable aid for a writer. A general page estimate is that there are 250–300 words to a printed page. It is generally accepted by publishers that specific word counts are necessary for different fiction genres; however this is changing with the event of digital publishing so please check publishers' guidelines. If you're self-publishing check bookstores and publishers but you are your own boss. Below are rough estimates. JOSH

* **Thriller:** 110,000+ words
* **Romantic category series:** 65–75,000 words
* **Literary/Commercial fiction:** 80–90,000+ words
* **Picture storybook:** 32 pages.
* **Junior fiction and non-fiction:** 8-11 year olds = 7000–30,000 words
* **Adolescent fiction and non-fiction:** 11-13 year olds = 7000–35,000 words
* **Young Adult:** (14+ resemble adult books) 20,000+ words
* **Novella:** 15,000 up to 60,000 words
* **Short stories:** Anything below 7500 words
* **Singles:** 3000 words

Keeping a word count as you write your first draft can be discouraging. You're probably taking two steps forward and one step back. Just write! Get that first draft down on paper. Worry about the word count later.

word-of-mouth marketing [See also Viral marketing]

Word-of-mouth marketing is marketing that is spread by the verbal recommendation of one person to another. PANDORA

Word-of-mouth marketing is being challenged by social media links.

word-of-the-week event [See also Dictionary/ Thesaurus]

Word-of-the-week event is a writerly sport for some writers' groups. Members post their newly found word-of-the-week on a notice board. Members enter a competition to see who knows the meaning. GINA

work-in-progress [See also Grasshopper writer]

Work-in-progress, aka WIP, is a writerly term referring to the novel you're working on at the moment. Be wary of discussing your work-in-progress—unless to other writers. Some writers work on more than one work-in-progress at a time. BILL

working on my novel [See also Procrastination/Work-in-progress]

Working on my novel is a phrase you will use constantly while you are writing your novel—creating something out of nothing. Working on my novel is a legitimate excuse to use for locking yourself in an attic while you dream, wait to be inspired, scribble or tap out pages and pages, edit and finally finish your novel. BILL

working title [See also Title]

A working title is the title you're using for your novel as you write. Don't spend too much time worrying about your title. Use your working title until inspiration strikes or a brilliant, must-buy title for your book is found by publishers, editors, agents or friends. BILL

Don't get hung-up about your working title. Most times it won't be the title you will finally choose.

worm [See also Backup]

Worm is a metaphor for a type of computer virus, which can spread on computers. A worm spreads quickly by itself. Use protection software if you're writing your novel on a computer. LEE

the wow factor [See also Branding/Marketing]

The Wow Factor is what agents and publishers are always looking for in a novel—a novel that ticks all the boxes. Authors who give thought to their readers and the marketability of their novel, could possibly be writing a novel with a *Wow* factor. PANDORA

write what you 'don't' know

Write what you *don't* know is advice rarely given to writers. But it makes sense. If you write what you *don't* know you will need to research, focus, and stretch your imagination. Writing what you *don't* know could prevent your family and friends becoming miffed, annoyed, and even traumatised by including them as recognisable characters in your novel. DAPHNE

> *You can always research what you need to know when you have finished writing what you don't know.*

write what you know

Write what you know is advice frequently given to writers. It makes sense. You don't have to do heaps of research when you rely on your life for inspiration and content when you are writing your novel. VIOLET

> *However, your life could make for a very limiting setting or plot. If this is the case use your imagination.*

writerly

Writerly is a word commonly used by writers. If you're writing a novel you can live a (mostly) blissful, writerly life—hopefully networking with lots of writerly friends. DIGBY

writer's block [See also Bad writing day/Brainstorming/Procrastination]

Writer's Block can appear as a huge hazard or a small pothole on the road to writing a novel. It can occur when you've arrived at the proverbial brick wall with your plot and don't know what to write next. Writers' Block may occur when you're caught in life-survival stuff and find it hard to return to your novel. Or it can occur when you're trapped in the minutiae of daily life and find it hard to connect with your novel. Don't worry. Writer's Block is not a terminal disease. It can be overcome. Try brainstorming. Try writing one sentence, then another and another. Or take time out and read a novel. This will inspire you, or make you determined to write a better novel. BILL

writers' centres

Writers' Centres are cool places run by writerly organisations to support writers. They are places—physical or online—where writers can network, attend workshops, and gain up-to-date book industry, self-publishing information, and other writerly assistance. LEE

Many Writers' Centres are subsided by government grants or you can become a member for a small fee.

writers' conferences

Writer's Conferences—aka festivals and events—come in all shapes, sizes and prices. Expensive conferences are not necessarily the best choice. The star-author might not hang around after his or her keynote speech to chat to writers. Prices can range from budget (a conference held in a small town with B&B accommodation) to a live-in conference held on an exotic island with high-end accommodation. Conferences can last from one to seven days and consist of sessions. Sessions cover a variety of bookish-type meetings and writerly activities. They can include panel discussions with agents and publishers, readings and talks by authors, and writers' workshops. Add-on features such as bookshops, book-signings and literary exhibitions make writers' conferences great places for a writer to hear and share information, goss, and trends in publishing. Professional manuscript assessments from a highly experienced editor or writer are often available at pre-arranged times and cost. Functions are also arranged where you can mix and mingle with fellow writers as well as agents, and publishing professionals. Check on the Internet for dates, times, places and costs of available conferences. LEE

> *A lone writer should aim to get to at least one writers' conference. Enjoy the buzz of being with writerly colleagues, book lovers and members of the book industry.*

writers' groups [See also Criticism/Feedback]

Writers' Groups can play an important part in a writer's life. If you hunt around you will find a group to match your personality, writing experience and writing genre e.g. crime, romance, commercial, literary fiction or a mix of writing and poetry. Even when you're a celeb author you can still meet regularly for professional and moral support. Celeb writers' groups usually agree to a code of silence re discussions and industry goss. Many writers choose a group with a mix of published and struggling writers, value their group and gain writerly support and advice at meetings. BIANCA

A practical example of writerly support and advice gained from a writers' group. If you don't put full stops inside quotation marks it can sabotage a sentence.

writers' guidelines [See also House style/Online slush pile]

Writers' Guidelines are formal statements of a publisher's submission and editorial needs, payment schedule, deadlines and other essential information. BILL

a writer's retreat [See also Sacrifice/Writing space]

A Writer's Retreat is a dream for most writers—a place set in an idyllic setting where you can write. It is somewhere to escape from the world complete with a pen, computer, printer, reams of paper and replacement inkjet cartridges. A writer's retreat can be a log cabin in a pine forest, a castle with an over-the-moat view, or a thatched cottage perched on a cliff-top overlooking the ocean. An ideal writer's retreat is a comfortable room with a desk, kettle, Internet connections and/or free wi-fi, home-cooked meals delivered to the door, good wine, blazing log fires, fans or aircon—depending on the weather. Constructive criticism provided by a resident writer-slash-caretaker could be an optional extra. There are retreats for writers run by state and literary organisations available to writers through grants. DAPHNE

A writer's retreat is just dream material for your average novel writer. Most writers write at home. Alone.

writing backwards [See also Crime Fiction/Ending]

Writing backwards is figuring out the ending of your novel and writing it first. It's a favourite writing method of mystery writers because the crime must be expanded in full in crime fiction and it's good to know who did what, and when. It is also comforting to have an idea of how your novel is going to end before you start your novel-writing journey. VIOLET

writing classes [See also NaNoWriMo]

Writing classes—also called creative writing classes, courses and workshops—are held at universities, colleges, and local community centres. They're great for disciplined writers who enjoy being in a classroom setting with set writing tasks, assignments, and deadlines. Short-term residential writing courses are a way to jump-start your novel. Check online, local libraries, and education faculties for classes, courses and venues. GINA

If you've already started your novel, a writers' group may be the answer for you.

writing-in-the-flow [See also Free writing/Inconsistencies]

Writing-in-the-flow is when you're caught up in your writing and it's flowing brilliantly. You know in your head what's going on, what has or hasn't happened to whom and when it's going to happen. When you revise watch out for gaps in your plot where you need further explanation for your readers as to what is happening to who, when and where. DAPHNE

writing process [See also Pantser/Plotter]

The writing process is the process you undertake to complete your novel. A writer will usually go through different writing stages in the process of writing their novel. These processes can include planning, researching, drafting, rewriting, and editing. It's a long, tough journey. Forget about getting published when you complete your novel. Your writing process should be its own joy and reward. If you can't hack the writing process—don't do it. VIOLET

Master positive inner dialogue. You can do it!

writing space [See also Writer's Retreat]

A writing space where you feel comfortable and can write is important for most writers. Many famous writers choose amazing places to write their novels—in the bath, their car, in bed, in a biggish cupboard, in a cafe—mostly due to necessity. Jane Austin wrote her five 80,000-word novels in the living room—with pen and ink! She covered her writing up whenever visitors called. Make sure your writing space is arranged ergonomically. For example, use a correct chair or back support. Keep a glass of water on your desk. If you're a beginning novel writer, forget the dream of having of a room-of-your-own. Just write! BIANCA

writing the second novel

Writing the second novel can be a struggle for most writers. There are many famous novelists who, after writing their best seller, were content to rest on their laurels. For example: Margaret Mitchell—*Gone with the Wind*, Anna Sewell—*Black Beauty*, Boris Pasternak—*Dr Zhivago*, and D.L. Salinger—*Catcher in the Rye.* DIGBY

If you only write one brilliant, fantastic novel that has impact on millions of people globally. Relax. You'll find some other work you can do. Hopefully you've been smart with your contract and can use your royalties to begin new projects.

X

X [See also Email]

X indicating *kiss* or *love* is used as a sign-off on e-mails. When communicating via emails to publishers or business colleagues be wary of using X or XX. The recipient could get the wrong idea. BIANCA

Xmas

Xmas is an abbreviation for Christmas. Some publishers, advertisers and newspapers avoid using the Christmas abbreviation *Xmas* for fear of offending readers. PANDORA

eXercise [See also Eyes]

eXercise is vital for writers. You need to break the hours you spend sitting in front of a computer—or the hours spent with a pencil and notebook—with movement. You need to be fit enough to keep writing novels in your old age. Amazingly a regular rhythmic exercise such as walking, or swimming laps—as well as being physically beneficial—can help you visualise what is coming next in your novel. VIOLET

Some members say an aerobic workout has the potential to keep you creating for the following two hours. This info has not been verified.

the X Factor [See also The Wow factor]

The X Factor is similar to the *Wow* factor. It's what your novel must have to break through to tired, exhausted, stressed (practically-burnt-out) agents, editors, and the reader struggling to read your novel while travelling on public transport. If you write with passion, originality, enthusiasm and confidence combined with great writing you'll have a fair chance of gaining the X Factor for your novel. JOSH

Y

YouTube [See also Book trailer/Social media]

You can place videos online through YouTube. Well produced videos—or not so well produced—can help to promote your novel. LEE

You're not a real writer...

You're not a real writer is a phrase that begins the adage—*You're not a real writer until you've been paid for your writing, or it's been published.* DIGBY

Members disagree with this adage but appreciate the fact that getting paid for your writing is essential if you want to put bread on the table and a roof over your head.

your/you're/yours

Your/You're/Yours can be confusing words for a writer.

* **Your** is the possessive adjective relating to you. For example: Do you have your manuscript with you?
* **You're** is a contraction of *you are*. For example: Digby said that you're (you are) coming to the writers' meeting.
* **Yours** is a possessive pronoun and does not have an apostrophe. For example: These bones are yours. GINA

Z

z

Z is the last letter in the alphabet. It is pronounced *zed* in Australia and the UK, and *zee* in the US. PANDORA

zero [See also Advance/Contract]

Zero is the cardinal number between +1 and -1. The plural of zero is zeros or zeroes. For example: There were many zeros in the advance payment for his novel. DIGBY

zombie fiction

Zombie fiction has become the new hot genre. Zombies are mindless minds—the living dead. Zombies can be a metaphor for a scary or terrifying threat. Zombies make great fodder for writers wishing to create and sustain suspense in their novels. There are many subgenres of Zombie fiction such as YA zombie series, Zombie erotica, Zombie science fiction, Steampunk, and even a subgenre of classics retold with horrific elements. *Pride and Prejudice and Zombies* was a runaway bestseller. BIANCA

Zombie fiction has huge potential. Why not bring a zombie to life in your next novel?

Essential Books for Your Library

Australian Handbook for Writers and Editors, 4th ed. A handbook that comprehensively covers the principles of grammar and punctuation, and the practice of common usage. (Margaret McKenzie, Woodslane Press)

The Chicago Manual of Style, 16th ed. The pre-eminent guide to publishing conventions in the US. It's a global publishing industry, the US and Australia have very different *rules* when it comes to style. (The University of Chicago Press)

Collins Australian Compact Dictionary. Easy to use. (HarperCollins Publishers)

Collins Dictionary for Writers and Editors. A comprehensive reference guide to words and usage, grammar and style conventions. (Martin Manser, HarperCollins Publishers)

Macquarie Dictionary. The go-to dictionary reference for Australian publishing. (John Wiley & Sons, Australia, Ltd)

Eats, Shoots & Leaves: The Zero tolerance approach to punctuation. Lyn Truss. Witty and chatty book by an English grammarian on proper grammar and punctuation. (Gotham)

The Editor's Companion 2nd ed. Explains the traditional skills for editing for publication. It is a recommended tool for editors, authors, traditional publishers and author-publishing. (Janet Mackenzie, Cambridge University Press)

The Elements of Style. 4th ed. William Strunk Jr. and E.B. White (Pearson) "No book in shorter space, with fewer words will help any writer more than this persistent little volume," says the Boston Globe.

On Writing: a Memoir of the Craft. Advice and reflections on the writing life by one of the best-selling authors of the time. Stephen King (Pocket Books)

The Penguin Working Words. An Australian Guide to Modern English Usage. Barry Hughes (Penguin)

Style Manual for Authors, Editors and Printers, 6th ed. The comprehensive Australian style manual for publishing professionals in both the public and private sectors. (John Wiley & Sons, Australia, Ltd)

Usage & Abusage. A Guide to Good English. Eric Partridge (Penguin Books)

Webster's American English Dictionary. Great to use when publishing to the US market. (Federal Street Press)

Members suggest writers have at least three dictionaries.

Index

I

X

Praise for *The Shelly Beach Writers' Group*

"An entrancing story."

WOMAN'S DAY

"A classic reinvention story with universally appealing ingredients."

DAILY TELEGRAPH

"Utterly charming… A sweet, funny and wise story."

WEEKEND GOLD COAST BULLETIN

"Best served with chardonnay and blinis with smoked salmon and sour cream."

SATURDAY AGE

"A warm and wonderful page-turner."

COUNTRY STYLE

www.ingramcontent.com/pod-product-compliance
Lightning Source LLC
Chambersburg PA
CBHW031217290326
41931CB00034B/180